Using Query/400

BY PATRICE GAPEN AND CATHERINE STOUGHTON

DUKE PRESS
A Division of
DUKE COMMUNICATIONS INTERNATIONAL
Loveland, Colorado

Library of Congress Cataloging-in-Publication Data

Gapen, Patrice.
Using Query/400 / by Patrice Gapen and Catherine Stoughton. — 1st ed.
p. cm.
Includes bibliographical references and index.
ISBN 1-882419-12-X
1. IBM AS/400 (Computer) — Programming 2. Database management.
3. Query/400. I. Stoughton, Catherine. II. Title.
QA76.8.I25919G357 1995
005. 74—dc20 94-44462
CIP

DUKE COMMUNICATIONS INTERNATIONAL
Loveland, Colorado

This book was printed and bound in the United States of America.

ISBN 1-882419-12-X

2 3 4 5 6 KP 9 8 7 6

To our families:
Herb and Sean Stoughton;
Rod, Megan, and Robin Southworth.
Thanks for your love and patience.

Acknowledgments

Our thanks to Sharon Hamm and Dave Bernard for editing this book, Dr. Judy Yeager of Western Michigan University for her technical review, Robin Strelow for the cover design, and Jan Caufman for her production work.

Special thanks to the Laramie County Community College Query/400 students who used, proofed, and made comments on the original versions of this text.

Table of Contents

Preface IX

Chapter 1: Using Query/400 1
- Objectives 1
- Introduction 1
- Files, Fields, and Record Formats 1
- Query Definitions 2
- Working with the Query Utility 2
- Specifying File Selections 3
- Saving and Exiting Query 5
- Running an Existing Query 7
- Review Questions 8
- Exercises 8

Chapter 2: Selecting and Sequencing Fields 9
- Objectives 9
- Introduction 9
- Selecting and Sequencing the Fields 10
- Review Questions 14
- Exercises 14

Chapter 3: Defining Result Fields 15
- Objectives 15
- Introduction 15
- Numeric Result Fields 17
- Character Result Fields 18
- Completing the Chapter Example Result Fields 19
- Review Questions 23
- Exercises 23

Chapter 4: Selecting Sort Fields To Resequence Output 25
- Objectives 25
- Introduction 25
- Selecting Fields for Sorting 25
- Review Questions 29
- Exercises 29

Chapter 5: Selecting Records for Reporting 31
- Objectives 31
- Introduction 31
- Comparison Tests 33
- Using AND/OR Comparisons 35

- Completing the Chapter Record Selection 36
- Review Questions 40
- Exercises 40

Chapter 6: Using Summary Functions 41
- Objectives 41
- Introduction 41
- Selecting the Report Summary Functions 41
- Review Questions 45
- Exercises 45

Chapter 7: Using Report Breaks 47
- Objectives 47
- Introduction 47
- Report Break Information 48
- Defining Report Breaks 49
- Review Questions 54
- Exercises 54

Chapter 8: Creating File Relationships 55
- Objectives 55
- Introduction 55
- Joining Files 56
- Review Questions 62
- Exercises 62

Chapter 9: Report Column Formatting 63
- Objectives 63
- Introduction 63
- Column Formatting 63
- Editing Numeric Fields 66
- Editing Date and Time Fields 68
- Review Questions 70
- Exercises 70

Chapter 10: Selecting Output Type and Form 71
- Objectives 71
- Introduction 71
- Printed Output Formatting 71
- Selecting Output for a Database File 76
- Review Questions 80
- Exercises 80

Appendix A: Data Files and the Display Physical File Command 81
The PAYMST File 81
The DPTMST File 81
The ADRMST File 82
Displaying Physical File Data on the AS/400 82

Appendix B: Collating Sequence and Processing Options 85
Selecting a Collating Sequence 85
Specifying Processing Options 85

Appendix C: Date Processing 87
Introduction 87
Converting a Numeric Date 87
Converting a Character Date 88
Examples of Date Operations 88

Index 91

Preface

The *Using Query/400* text focuses on Query/400 functions and the most commonly used menu items. The authors have attempted to shorten and simplify complex and advanced AS/400 functions. Technical users will note that they should reference other manuals for the exact use and definitions. For example, create authorities are discussed briefly in Chapter 10. This text does not intend to explore fully the topic of file authorities but does offer a short description of a few of the common options. The authors' intent is to provide the unfamiliar user with a step-by-step approach to the Query/400 menu so that Query/400 may be used to increase productivity both in the classroom and in the business environment. To that end, the sample files provided in Appendix A have a small number of records and represent "real world" examples. The text assumes that each student will either copy or create the three data files in a library that is dedicated to his or her own use. Thus, all the library references are denoted as "yourname". The authors strongly recommend that students complete every chapter example, because each subsequent chapter assumes the previous examples have been saved in the student's library; new chapters build upon the previous chapters' examples.

This text does assume that the user has some minimal knowledge of AS/400 hardware and operating software. Specifically, the text assumes that students are able to print from their print queue and that a printer is available. Also, students are expected to have access to and understand the purpose of the command line, and know where the attention key is on their particular keyboard. Keyboards vary depending on the terminal type, whether or not a personal computer is used, and what keyboard mapping was selected by the system administrator. The following substitutions are suggested for PC users, but other replacements may be required on each particular system.

QUERY/400 TEXT REFERENCE	PC USERS
Field Exit key	Right Ctrl key or Tab
Shift/Roll Up keys	Page Down
Shift/Roll Down keys	Page Up

How to Work with this Text

This text will use a payroll master file, PAYMST; an address master file, ADRMST; and a department master file, DPTMST, for its examples and exercises. These files should be in your library or in a library that you can access. Your instructor will provide this information to you. See Appendix A for information about these files, their fields, and their record formats.

In each chapter of this book you will create a Query report using a new technique. The end-of-chapter exercises will give you more practice using the concepts you have learned in that and previous chapters. Please use the file names given in the text for the queries you create, because later chapters will use previously created queries.

This text is based on Version 3 Release 1 of the AS/400 operating system. For more information on Query, see the *Query/400 User's Guide* (SC41-9614).

Chapter 1

Using Query/400

Objectives:

✓ To learn about Query/400

✓ To learn how to create, run, and save a Query definition

✓ To learn how to run an existing Query definition

Introduction

Query/400 is an IBM-licensed program that can be used to obtain information from any database file that has been defined on the AS/400. Query is used to select, arrange, and analyze this stored data to produce reports and other data files. Query definitions are created, run, and saved through a series of menus with prompts. You define to Query the input data and the output format, and whether the output should be displayed, printed, or sent to another database file. Many queries may exist for the same input file.

You can create Query definitions with varying degrees of complexity to access data. Query provides an easy and fast method to define the requirements for a report. Query can be used to obtain information from one file or from a combined set of up to 32 files. With Query, you can select from one to all fields and organize them into a report or another file. Record selection tests provide the flexibility to have only selected records included in the output.

Files, Fields, and Record Formats

Most data on the AS/400 is organized into objects called database files. Each file contains records, and each record contains fields organized by record format. For example, a company's payroll file would contain a record for each employee. Each employee's record would have fields such as employee ID, name, salary amount, department, and so on. Each record would contain different data, because each employee is different; but each record would be organized in the same format.

Query uses these files, fields, and record formats, together with the options you develop, to produce a report or file. Query "reads" the records in the file for you. All you have to specify is the definition of the output: how the data is to be selected, arranged, and formatted.

Query Definitions

You will use the Work with Query (WRKQRY) command to start Query/400. Through a series of screen displays you will define a file and the actions you want to use on the file's records. While you are defining your Query, you will be able to run it interactively to see your report. When you exit Query, you can save this definition. A Query definition is an AS/400 object (type *QRYDFN) that contains the file information, record selection, field and record arrangement, and report format details. This object is saved in a designated library. You can run this Query definition again when the data has changed, just as you would run any RPG or COBOL program with new data.

Working with the Query Utility

The goal of this chapter's exercise will be to create, display, and print a report from the PAYMST physical file. The Query report will list the data in the order that the records are sequenced in the file (arrival sequence). The fields in a PAYMST record are employee identification number, department number, employee name, and monthly salary.

To begin Query, you must first access the Query Utility menu:

Type	**WRKQRY**	on any command line
Press	**Enter**	

Figure 1.1 shows the Work with Queries menu.

Figure 1.1
Work with Queries Menu

```
                               Work with Queries

Type choices, press Enter.

  Option . . . . _            1=Create, 2=Change, 3=Copy, 4=Delete
                              5=Display, 6=Print definition
                              8=Run in batch, 9=Run
  Query  . . . . __________   Name, F4 for list
    Library. . . yourname     Name, *LIBL, F4 for list




F3=Exit          F4=Prompt          F5=Refresh          F12=Cancel
```

To begin a new query, use the Create function. It is not necessary to enter a name on this screen when creating a new query.

Type	**1**	to create a new query
Press	**Enter**	

Specifying File Selections

When you specify the Create option, you are shown the Define the Query display (Figure 1.2). This is where you will select up to 11 options to define your query. The first thing you must do is to define the name of the input file(s) that Query will be using. This is the only mandatory item needed to produce a report from Query. You can select the other options in any order, because each is a separate process. However, the options are shown in a sequence that is a dependent relationship. You will see this relationship develop as you work through the text. You can modify options at any time after they are initially selected.

Notice in Figure 1.2 that Query has placed a "1" in the options column on the Specify file selections line. You must now select this option:

Press **Enter** to choose the Specify file selection option

Figure 1.2
Define the Query Screen

```
                              Define the Query

Query . . . . :                          Option . . . . CREATE
  Library . . :      yourname

Type options, press Enter.  Press F21 to select all.
  1=Select

Opt         Query Definition Option
 1          Specify file selections
 _          Define result fields
 _          Select and sequence fields
 _          Select records
 _          Select sort fields
 _          Select collating sequence
 _          Specify report column formatting
 _          Select report summary functions
 _          Define report breaks
 _          Select output type and output form
 _          Specify processing options

F3=Exit          F5=Report                 F12=Cancel
F13=Layout       F18=Files                 F21=Select all
```

You are now at the Specify File Selections screen (Figure 1.3), where you can specify one or more database files that you want your query to read. This example will use only one file. We will discuss multiple file relationships in Chapter 8.

Use the physical file name PAYMST as the input file name for Figure 1.3.

Type **PAYMST** as the file name

If PAYMST is in your library, you will accept the remaining default options. If PAYMST is not in your library, type the correct library name before pressing Enter.

Press **Enter** to accept the remaining default options

Figure 1.3
Specify File Selections Screen

```
                              Specify File Selections

Type choices, press Enter.  Press F9 to specify an additional file selection.

File . . . . . . . .  __________         Name, F4 for list
  Library . . . . .     yourname         Name, *LIBL, F4 for list
Member . . . . . . .  *FIRST             Name, *FIRST, F4 for list
Format . . . . . . .  *FIRST             Name, *FIRST, F4 for list










F3=Exit           F4=Prompt          F5=Report          F9=Add file
F12=Cancel        F13=Layout         F24=More keys
```

If you have made an error in the library or file name, you will receive an error message. Correct the library or file name to continue. Query will display the following message to verify the correct file name and library:

```
Select file(s), or press Enter to confirm.
```

Press **Enter** when the file information is correct

Figure 1.4 shows that the system will return to the Define the Query menu.

Because an input file has now been defined, the 1 has been removed from the option column. A greater-than sign (>) has appeared before the Specify file selections. The greater-than sign indicates that this item has been designated. As other options are chosen, each will be marked with the greater-

Figure 1.4
Define the Query Menu

```
                                Define the Query

Query . . . . :                        Option . . . . CREATE
  Library . . :      yourname

Type options, press Enter.  Press F21 to select all.
  1=Select

Opt           Query Definition Option
 _          > Specify file selections
 _            Define result fields
 _            Select and sequence fields
 _            Select records
 _            Select sort fields
 _            Select collating sequence
 _            Specify report column formatting
 _            Select report summary functions
 _            Define report breaks
 _            Select output type and output form
 _            Specify processing options

F3=Exit           F5=Report
F13=Layout        F18=Files                  F21=Select all
Select options, or press F3 to save or run the query
```

than sign. Query will return to this menu after each option has been accessed.

Remember that Specify file selections is the only required option. Note the system message at the bottom of the screen: Select options, or press F3 to save or run the query. With the file defined, other options can now be defined. To select other options, place a "1" in the options column on the line you wish to select. If you press the F3 key, you will exit the Query definition and be given options for saving and running the query. You will use the F3 key when you have completed your query definition and want to save it, or if you want to save the query and run it in batch. You also can use the F3 key if you need to exit Query without saving the definition.

You will use the F5 key to interactively run a query to display on the screen. You can use this key within all the Query options. You do not have to be on the Define the Query menu to run a report to the screen. You can run a report each time you add another option to your Query definition.

Press **F5** to interactively run the report to your screen

The sequence of the data in the report is the same sequence as the data in the PAYMST file. Pressing F5 causes the report to appear, which is shown in Figure 1.5.

Figure 1.5
Display Report Screen

```
                              Display Report
                                                          Report width . . .53
Position to line . . .  ______          Shift to column  . . . . . ._
Line          ....+....1....+....2....+....3....+....4....+....5....+..
              EMP ID  DEPT NO   EMPLOYEE NAME        MONTHLY SALARY
000001          1234     400    JONES, BILL                1,322.00
000002          3567     600    SMITHE, CAROL              1,567.75
000003          5632     200    GREEN, TOM                 1,200.00
000004          2567     100    ADAMS, MARK                1,546.50
000005          4672     600    BLACKBERG, KAREN           1,300.00
000006          7290     400    KLEIN, JOHN                1,400.00
000007          1892     500    TUCKER, MARY               1,500.00
000008          0516     400    WALKER, GARY               1,775.25
000009          6340     100    POWERS, SUSAN              1,725.00
000010          5718     300    HART, BOB                  1,222.00
******     ******  End of report  ******

                                                                     Bottom
F3=Exit    F12=Cancel    F19=Left    F20=Right    F21=Split
```

Press **F12** to exit the Display Report screen and return to the Define the Query screen

Saving and Exiting Query

You will now save this simple Query definition. Once a Query definition has been saved, you can access the definition at any time. You can also change the definition and save it with a new format.

Press	**F3**	to access the save and exit screen

The screen shown in Figure 1.6 will be displayed.

Figure 1.6
Exit Query Screen

```
                              Exit this Query

Type choices, press Enter.

  Save definition . . . . .   Y                Y=Yes, N=No

  Run Option  . . . . . . .   1                1=Run interactively
                                               2=Run in Batch
                                               3=Do not run

  For a saved definition:
    Query . . . . . . . . .   __________       Name
      Library . . . . . . .   yourname         Name, F4 for list

    Text  . . . . . . . . .   ______________________________

  Authority . . . . . . . .   *LIBCRTAUT       *LIBCRTAUT, *CHANGE,
                                               *ALL, *EXCLUDE,
                                               *USE, authorized
                                               list name

F4=Prompt           F5=Report           F12=Cancel     F13=Layout
F14=Define the query
```

When saving files and exiting Query, you have three run options:

1. You can run your Query definition interactively again, with the output displaying on the screen. You should be aware that running large Query reports interactively can significantly degrade system performance.

2. You can have your Query definition run in batch mode so that you have a printed report in your output queue.

3. You can specify that your Query definition not be run.

Change this Query definition to run in batch mode so you will have a printed report:

Press	**Tab** (or **New Line**)	to bypass the "Y" and save the definition
Type	**2**	as the Run Option, for batch
Type	**paymstq1**	as the save name for this first query using PAYMST
Press	**Field Exit**	to exit the name field
Press	**Tab**	to bypass the library. You want to have the definition stored in your library.
Type	**PAYMST Query - arrival sequence**	as the Text information
Press	**Enter**	to save and run the Query report

You will return to the Work with Queries menu. You will receive a message that your batch job has completed normally. The Query report will be in your output queue with the name QPQUPRFIL. The report contains two pages: The first page is a header page with information about the query, including its name and the library where it is stored; the second page is the report.

Query definitions do not have to be saved. You may have received your query answer interactively, or you may have made a major error and want to quit and start over. To exit Query without saving, use F3 to exit the Define the Query menu. On the Exit this Query screen, type an N to not save the definition, and a 3 to not run the definition. Press Enter.

Running an Existing Query

When you saved the Query definition with the name PAYMSTQ1, you created an object with that name in your library. This definition can now be run when you are in Query, or when you are in PDM (Programming Development Manager).

To access a saved definition through Query, you need to begin at the Work with Queries menu. (Type **wrkqry** on any command line — see Figure 1.1 for reference.) Type a 9 as the option, and the name of the query you want to run. If you do not remember the name of your query, press F4 on the name line, and all the queries in your library will be listed for you to choose from.

To access a saved definition through PDM, you need to be on your Work with Objects Using PDM screen. (Type **wrkobjpdm** on any command line.) Query definitions have a type of *QRYDFN. You will use option 16 to run a query definition in PDM.

Review Questions

1. What is the mandatory definition for Query to generate a report?
2. Why would a programmer want to learn Query?
3. Why would a user want to learn Query?
4. How do you exit Query without saving the definition? Why would you want to do this?

Exercises

1. Print the report that was created in this chapter.
2. Create a Query definition to list the DPTMST file. Save your file with the name CH1EX2 and a meaningful text name. Print the report.
3. Create a Query definition to list the ADRMST file. Save your file with the name CH1EX3 and a meaningful text name. Print the report.

Chapter 2

Selecting and Sequencing Fields

Objectives:

- ✓ To learn how to change the sequence of the fields that are printed in a Query report
- ✓ To learn how to print only certain fields from a record

Introduction

This chapter describes how to select and re-arrange the fields that will appear on a Query report. The Query default is that all fields in the record(s) of the selected file(s) will be printed. The Select and sequence fields option allows for fields to be selected and then printed in any order across the page. Query can select and sequence a maximum of 500 fields.

The chapter exercise will create a new Query definition for the PAYMST physical file. Remember that to begin Query you must first access the Query Utility menu:

Type	**WRKQRY**	on any command line
Press	**Enter**	
Type	**1**	to create a new query
Press	**Enter**	
Press	**Enter**	to choose the Specify file selections option

Select the PAYMST file.

Type	**PAYMST**	as the file name
Press	**Enter**	
Press	**Enter**	to confirm

Referencing Figure 2.1, the Define the Query menu,

Type	**1**	to choose the Select and sequence fields option
Press	**Enter**	

You will now be at the Select and Sequence Fields screen (Figure 2.2).

Figure 2.1
Define the Query Menu

```
                              Define the Query

Query . . . . :                          Option . . . . CREATE
  Library . . :       yourname

Type options, press Enter.  Press F21 to select all.
  1=Select

Opt          Query Definition Option
 _         > Specify file selections
             Define result fields
 1           Select and sequence fields
 _           Select records
 _           Select sort fields
 _           Select collating sequence
 _           Specify report column formatting
 _           Select report summary functions
 _           Define report breaks
 _           Select output type and output form
 _           Specify processing options

F3=Exit          F5=Report
F13=Layout       F18=Files                 F21=Select all
Select options, or press F3 to save or run the query.
```

Figure 2.2
Select and Sequence Fields Screen

```
                        Select and Sequence Fields

Type sequence number (0-9999) for the names of up to 500 fields
  to appear in the report, press Enter.

Seq          Field
____         EMPID
____         DEPTNO
____         NAME
____         MONSAL

                                                                  Bottom
F3=Exit        F5=Report       F11=Display        F12=Cancel
F13=Layout     F20=Renumber    F21=Select all     F24=More keys
```

Selecting and Sequencing the Fields

The written request for the query states this new report should not include the employee ID, and the name must be the first field, followed by the department number and the salary. Therefore, the fields must be sequenced to define this request. To sequence the fields, type a number before each field that will be printed in the report. The lowest sequence number indicates the first field in the report, and the highest sequence number indicates the last field, left to right. Leave the Sequence number area blank to omit a field.

Type	**the sequence numbers**	as shown in Figure 2.3, leaving EMPID blank. Use the Field Exit key to move from field to field.
Press	**Enter**	

Figure 2.3
Select and Sequence Fields Screen — Sequence Numbers Selected

```
                              Select and Sequence Fields
Type sequence number (0-9999) for the names of up to 500 fields to appear in the
 report, press Enter.

Seq          Field
____         EMPID
2___         DEPTNO
1___         NAME
3___         MONSAL






F3-Exit        F5-Report        F11-Display        F12-Cancel
F13-Layout     F20-Renumber     F21-Select all     F24-More keys
```

Query will re-arrange the fields in the order that you have requested and request that you confirm these selections. See Figure 2.4 for an example of verification of your selection.

TIP: F20 will resequence the fields to allow other fields to be inserted. For example, if the requirements change and EMPID should now be printed between DEPTNO and NAME, you would first need to press F20 to resequence the numbers as 10, 20, and 30. Then you could type 15 in the EMPID sequence column to insert its position between DEPTNO and NAME. The remaining fields would be moved.

Press **Enter** to accept the sequence as shown in Figure 2.4

Figure 2.4
Select and Sequence Fields Screen — Sequence Verified

```
                              Select and Sequence Fields
Type sequence number (0-9999) for the names of up to 500 fields to appear in the
report, press Enter.

Seq          Field
___1         NAME
___2         DEPTNO
___3         MONSAL
____         EMPID





                                                                      Bottom
F3-Exit          F5-Report          F11-Display          F12-Cancel
F13-Layout       F20-Renumber       F21-Select all       F24-More keys
Press Enter to confirm.
```

Figure 2.5 shows your return to the Define the Query menu; note that the greater-than sign appears in front of the completed items.

Figure 2.5
Define the Query Menu

```
                               Define the Query

Query . . . . :                                  Option . . . . CREATE
  Library . . :        yourname

Type options, press Enter.  Press F21 to select all.
  1=Select

Opt          Query Definition Option
 _         > Specify file selections
 _           Define result fields
 _         > Select and sequence fields
 _           Select records
 _           Select sort fields
 _           Select collating sequence
 _           Specify report column formatting
 _           Select report summary functions
 _           Define report breaks
 _           Select output type and output form
 _           Specify processing options

F3=Exit          F5=Report
F13=Layout       F18=Files                 F21=Select all
Select options, or press F3 to save or run the query.
```

Display this report.

Press **F5** to interactively run the report to your screen

See Figure 2.6 for an example of the report display.

Figure 2.6
Report Display Screen

```
                              Display Report
                                                    Report width . . .57
Position to line . . . _____      Shift to column  . . . . . . ._
Line     ....+....1....+...2....+....3....+....4....+....5....+..
         EMPLOYEE NAME         DEPT NO  MONTHLY SALARY
000001   JONES, BILL           400          1,322.00
000002   SMITHE, CAROL         600          1,567.75
000003   GREEN, TOM            200          1,200.00
000004   ADAMS, MARK           100          1,546.50
000005   BLACKBERG, KAREN      600          1,300.00
000006   KLEIN, JOHN           400          1,400.00
000007   TUCKER, MARY          500          1,500.00
000008   WALKER, GARY          400          1,775.25
000009   POWERS, SUSAN         100          1,725.00
000010   HART, BOB             300          1,222.00
******   ********  End of report  ******

                                                              Bottom
F3=Exit     F12=Cancel     F19=Left        F20=Right       F21=Split
```

Press **F12** to clear the display when you have compared your display to the text

Press **F3** to access the save and exit screen

Press	**Tab**	to bypass the "Y"
Type	**2**	as the Run Option
Type	**paymstq2**	as the query save name
Press	**Field Exit**	
Press	**Tab**	to bypass the library
Type	**PAYMST Query with EMPID omitted**	as the Text information
Press	**Enter**	to save and run the Query report

The Query report will be on your output queue with the name QPQUPRFIL.

Review Questions

1. Explain why a user might want certain fields omitted from a report.
2. Explain how to drop one or more fields from a Query report.
3. Explain how to place a field back into a Query report after the field has been omitted.
4. Explain why a user might wish to have fields displayed in a different sequence than is in the file.

Exercises

1. Use the DPTMST file and print a report with only the Department Name. Save this report as CH2EX1.
2. Use the DPTMST file and print a report with the fields in the following sequence: Department Name, Department Number, and Annual Budget. Save this report as CH2EX2.
3. Use the ADRMST file and print a report with the fields in the following sequence: State, Zip, Employee ID, and Street. Save this report as CH2EX3.
4. Use the PAYMST file and print a report with the following fields: Department Number, Employee ID, and Monthly Salary. Save this report as CH2EX4.

Chapter 3

Defining Result Fields

Objectives:

- ✓ To learn how to create new fields through numeric and alphanumeric operations
- ✓ To learn how to use the arithmetic operators
- ✓ To learn how to use the character operators

Introduction

This chapter will describe how to define and use new fields, based on fields that exist in your selected file(s). These result fields can be created from actions on either numeric or character data fields. For example, you may need to print a social security number with hyphens or to print the result of multiplying two fields. Both of these actions require new fields to be created.

Date and time manipulations are also available in Query. See Appendix C for date processing functions and operations.

The following exercise will produce a report to evaluate the cost of providing the employees in the PAYMST file with a 5 percent raise. Each employee's current salary and the employee's proposed salary will need to be displayed to provide management with adequate information for decision making.

To begin, access Query and select the PAYMST file.

This report requires that a new field, called a result field, be created to calculate each employee's 5 percent raise. The Define result fields option must be selected.

Referencing Figure 3.1, the Define the Query menu,

Type	1	to select Define result fields
Press	**Enter**	

TIP: Remember that Query does not change the data stored in the field. Only the display of the field is modified by the Query options.

The Define Result Fields screen is shown in Figure 3.2.

Figure 3.1
Define the Query Menu

```
                              Define the Query

Query . . . . :                        Option . . . . CREATE
  Library . . :       yourname

Type options, press Enter.  Press F21 to select all.
  1=Select

Opt         Query Definition Option
 _        > Specify file selections
 _          Define result fields
 _          Select and sequence fields
 _          Select records
 _          Select sort fields
 _          Select collating sequence
 _          Specify report column formatting
 _          Select report summary functions
 _          Define report breaks
 _          Select output type and output form
 _          Specify processing options

F3=Exit           F5=Report
F13=Layout        F18=Files                  F21=Select all
Select options, or press F3 to save or run the query.
```

Figure 3.2
Define Result Fields Menu

```
                          Define Result Fields

Type definitions using field names or constants and operators,
    press Enter.  Operators:  +, -, *, /, SUBSTR, ||, DATE...

Field     Expression                    Column Heading              Len     Dec
______    _________________________     ________________________    ___     ___
          _________________________     ________________________
          _________________________     ________________________
______    _________________________     ________________________    ___     ___
          _________________________     ________________________
          _________________________     ________________________
                                                                         Bottom
...............................................................................
Field     Column Heading                                            Len     Dec
EMPID     EMP ID                                                      4
DEPTNO    DEPT NO                                                     3
NAME      EMPLOYEE NAME                                              20
MONSAL    MONTHLY SALARY                                              6       2

                                                                         Bottom
F3=Exit        F5=Report      F9=Insert          F11=Display names
F12=Cancel     F13=Layout     F20=Reorganize     F24=More keys
```

TIP: If your screen does not show the expanded field information (column heading, length, and decimals), press F11 to display this data.

TIP: If all the fields do not fit on the screen, you will see the familiar "More..." Press Shift/Roll Up and use the cursor to display the remaining fields.

Figure 3.2 shows a split screen. The top portion is for defining the new field information. A unique new field name must be established for each new result field. This variable name must be different than any other existing field name. This result field name must begin with an alphabetic character (A-Z, $, #, or @) and must be no longer than 9 alphanumeric characters (A-Z, 0-9, $, #, @, or _). There can be no embedded blanks in the result field name.

You can use either a numeric or character expression to create this new field. A numeric expression uses numeric variables and/or constants with the +, -, *, and / operators. A character expression uses character variables and/or constants with the concatenation (||) or substring (SUBSTR) operators.

If a column heading is not provided, the result field name will be used as the column heading. You can specify up to three lines of 20 characters each for a column heading. *NONE should be specified if no column heading is desired.

You do not need to define the length of the new result field; Query will determine the length for you. However, numeric result fields will include the total number of decimal positions. For example, if you multiply two fields that each have two decimal positions, the result field will have four decimal positions. Character result fields must have length (Len) and decimal (Dec) areas blank.

The lower portion of the screen in Figure 3.2 contains a list of the field names from your selected file(s). This lower portion of the screen is for your convenience so you do not have to remember which fields are within the input record, or how the field names are spelled. The expanded field information shows which fields are character and which are numeric.

Numeric Result Fields

A numeric result field is calculated using the available numeric operators with numeric fields or constants. For example, a field named `payrate` might be multiplied by a field named `hours` to give gross pay. In this example, the result field name would be `gross` and the expression would be `payrate*hours`. Another example would be to multiply a numeric field by a constant. For example, an hourly quota would be multiplied by 8 to give the quota for the shift. In this example, the result field name might be `qtasft` and the expression would be `qtahr*8`. Conversely, the quota for the shift could be divided by 8 to provide the quota for an hour. The expression would then be `qtasft/8`. The following example shows how these three examples would be typed on a Define Result Fields screen.

Field	Expression
GROSS	PAYRATE*HOURS
QTASFT	QTAHR*8
QTAHR	QTASFT/8

The length of a numeric field is the total number of positions to the left and right of the decimal point, not including the decimal point. Decimal positions are the number of digits to the right of the decimal point, and a whole number must have decimal positions of zero. Query will determine the length for you, but you may lengthen or shorten an output field by using length and decimal. Remember that Query sums the decimal positions in multiplication operations. If payrate was defined as 4.2 and hours defined with a length of 3.1, gross would have a defined length of 7.3.

TIP: If you define a numeric result field with an inadequate length, the report will show the field filled with plus signs (+). Query also rounds the decimal position according to the system defaults. See Appendix B for more information.

TIP: By pressing the F13 key (Layout), you will see the format of the query depicted with Xs for character fields and 9s for numeric fields.

Character Result Fields

Character fields may be separated (substring) and combined (concatenated) on the Define the Result Fields screen. The substring operation allows you to extract a piece from a character field. For example, a phone number is usually stored as 10 characters, with the area code as the first three digits. If all the records are within the same area code, it is not necessary to print the area code. The area code may be dropped from printing with the substring (**SUBSTR**) command. SUBSTR has the following format:

SUBSTR(Field Name, Beginning Position, Length of substring)

In the area code example, if the result field were PHONE7 and the existing field name were PHONE, the expression would be

Field	Expression
PHONE7	SUBSTR(PHONE,4,7)

This translates to the following: Beginning in the fourth position of the 10-character field named PHONE, extract that fourth character along with the following six characters. Those seven characters would then be assigned to a new result field name, PHONE7.

The second character operation is a process of joining two or more fields or constants together to create a new field. This process is termed **concatenation.** Two vertical bar symbols are the operator for concatenation. The format for concatenation is

field name (or constant) || field name (or constant) ...

The PHONE7 field that was just created with the substring command will be used in a concatenation example. A request has been made that this new seven-character phone number be printed with a hyphen between the third and fourth characters (xxx-xxxx). This means that PHONE7 will have to be "pulled apart" into two additional result fields, and put back together with the intervening hyphen. To include any constant, the constant must be enclosed in single quote marks ('). To print the hyphen as a constant in the phone number, you must enter it as '-'. Three steps are required to accomplish this task. See the example below for a partial screen of result fields.

Field	Expression
PHONE3	SUBSTR(PHONE7,1,3)
PHONE4	SUBSTR(PHONE7,4,4)
NEWPHONE	PHONE3 || '-' || PHONE4

PHONE3 becomes the first three characters of the seven-character PHONE field. PHONE4 becomes the last four characters of the seven-character PHONE field. NEWPHONE re-assembles the first three characters, followed by a hyphen, followed by the last four characters. The result, called NEWPHONE, is the usual method for printing a phone number; for example, 555-1234.

TIP: You can omit the length parameter in the SUBSTR command if the length is from the beginning position to the end of the field.

TIP: You cannot define the length of a new character field on the Define Result Fields screen. Character field length is changed on the Specify Report Column Formatting display. See Chapter 9.

Completing the Chapter Example Result Fields

Continue working on your Query definition for the 5 percent raise. The new salary field name will be NEWSAL; the expression will be the monthly salary times the constant 1.05; the column heading will be "NEW SALARY"; and the new field should be a length of 6 positions with 2 decimals. See Figure 3.3 for the correct entries.

Type	**NEWSAL**	as the field name
Press	**Field Exit**	
Type	**MONSAL*1.05**	as the expression to calculate the 5 percent pay increase
Press	**Field Exit**	
Type	**NEW SALARY**	as the column heading
Press	**Field Exit**	
Type	**6**	as the length
Press	**Field Exit**	
Type	**2**	as the number of decimals
Press	**Enter**	

After accepting these Define Result Field entries, you will return to the Define the Query menu. A greater-than sign has been placed before the Define result fields line. The result fields are now defined and you can generate the report.

Figure 3.3
Define Result Fields Screen

```
                              Define Result Fields

Type definitions using field names or constants and operators,
    press Enter.  Operators:  +, -, *, /, SUBSTR, ||, DATE...

Field      Expression               Column Heading        Len     Dec
NEWSAL      MONSAL*1.05             NEW SALARY              6       2

                                                                    Bottom
...........................................................................
Field      Expression                                     Len     Dec
EMPID      EMP ID                                           4
DEPTNO     DEPT NO                                          3
NAME       EMPLOYEE NAME                                   20
MONSAL     MONTHLY SALARY                                   6       2

                                                                    Bottom
F3=Exit        F5=Report       F9=Insert          F11=Display names
F12=Cancel     F13=Layout      F20=Reorganize     F24=More keys
```

Press **F5** to interactively run the report to your screen

The report displayed on your screen should match Figure 3.4.

Figure 3.4
Display Report Screen

```
                              Display Report
                                                       Report width . . .65
Position to line . . . ______      Shift to column  . . . . . .__
Line       ....+....1....+....2....+....3....+....4....+....5....+..
           NEW SALARY  EMP ID  DEPT NO  EMPLOYEE NAME     MONTHLY SAL
000001       1,388.10   1234   400      JONES, BILL          1,322.00
000002       1,646.14   3567   600      SMITHE, CAROL        1,567.75
000003       1,260.00   5632   200      GREEN, TOM           1,200.00
000004       1,623.83   2567   100      ADAMS, MARK          1,546.50
000005       1,365.00   4672   600      BLACKBERG, KAREN     1,300.00
000006       1,470.00   7290   400      KLEIN, JOHN          1,400.00
000007       1,575.00   1892   500      TUCKER, MARY         1,500.00
000008       1,864.01   0516   400      WALKER, GARY         1,775.25
000009       1,811.25   6340   100      POWERS, SUSAN        1,725.00
000010       1,283.10   5718   300      HART, BOB            1,222.00
******     ********  End of report  ******

                                                                    Bottom
F3=Exit      F12=Cancel      F19=Left      F20=Right        F21=Split
```

The report has calculated the increase in salary. However, the new field was placed at the beginning of a report line. The report would look much better if the new field were at the end of the line. To correct this, you need to access the Select and sequence fields option to reposition the fields.

Press **F12** to clear the report and return to the Define the Query menu
Type **1** to choose the Select and sequence fields option
Press **Enter**

Figure 3.5
Select and Sequence Fields Screen

```
                              Select and Sequence Fields

Type sequence number (0-9999) for the names of up to 500 fields to appear in the
  report, press Enter.

Seq          Field
____         NEWSAL
____         EMPID
____         DEPTNO
____         NAME
____         MONSAL







                                                                        Bottom
F3=Exit        F5=Report        F11=Display        F12=Cancel
F13=Layout     F20=Renumber     F21=Select all     F24=More keys
```

You will now be at the Select and sequence fields screen. (Figure 3.5.)

Type	**5**	for NEWSAL
Press	**Field Exit**	
Type	**1**	for EMPID
Press	**Field Exit**	
Type	**2**	for DEPTNO
Press	**Field Exit**	
Type	**3**	for NAME
Press	**Field Exit**	
Type	**4**	for MONSAL
Press	**Field Exit**	
Press	**Enter**	
Press	**Enter**	to confirm the sequence numbers
Press	**F5**	to display a reformatted report

Check your display against Figure 3.6 on page 22.

Figure 3.6
Display Report Screen

```
                                   Display Report
                                                                 Report width . . .65
Position to line . . . _______     Shift to column  . . . . . .__
Line      ....+....1....+....2....+....3....+....4....+....5....+..
          EMP ID  DEPT NO  EMPLOYEE NAME  MONTHLY SALARY NEW SALARY
000001     1234     400    JONES, BILL       1,322.00      1,388.10
000002     3567     600    SMITHE, CAROL     1,567.75      1,646.14
000003     5632     200    GREEN, TOM        1,200.00      1,260.00
000004     2567     100    ADAMS, MARK       1,546.50      1,623.83
000005     4672     600    BLACKBERG, KAREN  1,300.00      1,365.00
000006     7290     400    KLEIN, JOHN       1,400.00      1,470.00
000007     1892     500    TUCKER, MARY      1,500.00      1,575.00
000008     0516     400    WALKER, GARY      1,775.25      1,864.01
000009     6340     100    POWERS, SUSAN     1,725.00      1,811.25
000010     5718     300    HART, BOB         1,222.00      1,283.10
******  ********  End of report  ******

                                                                           Bottom
F3=Exit     F12=Cancel     F19=Left        F20=Right       F21=Split
```

Press	**F12**	to clear the report
Press	**F3**	to begin the save
Press	**Tab**	to bypass the "Y"
Type	**2**	as the Run Option
Type	**paymstq3**	as the query name
Press	**Field Exit**	
Press	**Tab**	to bypass the library
Type	**PAYMST Query with result field NEWSAL**	as the Text information
Press	**Enter**	to save and run the Query report
Press	**F3**	to return to the Query Utility Menu

The Query report will be in your output queue with the name QPQUPRFIL.

Review Questions

1. Explain the purpose of result fields.
2. What character operators may be used with character fields to create a result field?
3. What arithmetic operators may be used with numeric fields to create a result field?
4. What is the purpose of the SUBSTR expression?
5. Why should column headings be assigned to a created field?
6. What is the maximum length of a result field variable name?

Exercises

1. Use the DPTMST file. Print a report with all the DPTMST fields, plus a new field where the first character of the department number is now the last character. For example, department 400 will print as 004. This new field must print as the last field. Save the report as CH3EX1.
2. Use the DPTMST file. Print a report with only the department number and the department name where the first three characters of the department name are deleted. The new name field should print first on the line. Save the report as CH3EX2.
3. Use the ADRMST file. Print a report with only the following four fields, in the sequence listed:

   phone number, formatted as
   XXX-XXX-XXXX
   street
   city, state, and zip code as one field, with one space between city and state, and state and zip
   employee ID

   The two new fields should have column headings of PHONE NUM and CITY-ST-ZIP. Save the report as CH3EX3.
4. Use the ADRMST file. Print two fields: employee ID and a combined field of zip code and the state. The new field should have a column heading of ZIP-ST. Save the report as CH3EX4.
5. Use the PAYMST file. Print two fields: employee name and multiply to display only 10 percent of the monthly salary. Save the report as CH3EX5.
6. Use the DPTMST file. Print all the fields, and include a new field that is the Annual Budget less 5 percent (or 95 percent of the Annual Budget). Save the report as CH3EX6.

Chapter 4

Selecting Sort Fields To Resequence Output

Objectives:

✓ To understand the process of sorting data

✓ To be able to print a report with the data in other than arrival sequence

Introduction

This chapter describes how fields are selected from the input record to control the sequence of the output. Until now the Query reports have been in arrival sequence, the sequence of the data in the input file. The Select sort field option in Query lets you choose one or more fields by which to resequence the output. The input data file remains in arrival sequence.

Files can be sorted on any one field or on several fields. For example, the PAYMST file can now be sorted in alphabetical sequence on employee name; the DPTMST file can be sorted in alphabetical sequence on department name; and the ADRMST file can be sorted in zip code sequence. You can use more than one field for sorting, so that an address file could be sorted by city name within state, and a sales file could be sorted by date of sale within department within store within state.

In this chapter exercise, the PAYMST file will be sorted by employee name within department number. To begin, access Query and select the PAYMST file.

Referencing Figure 4.1, the Define the Query menu,

Type	1	to choose the Select sort fields option
Press	**Enter**	

You will now be at the Select sort fields screen (Figure 4.2).

Selecting Fields for Sorting

A priority is assigned to the field or fields that will resequence the records in the file for the report. A sort priority number is assigned to each field that will be sorted. If more than one field will be used for the sort, the major sort field is assigned the lowest value. For example, to sort all cities alphabetically within states, the state field would be the major sort field, and it would be assigned the lowest number. The city field would be considered the minor

Figure 4.1
Define the Query Menu

```
                              Define the Query

Query . . .                                     Option . . . . CREATE
  Library . .   yourname

Type options, press Enter.  Press F21 to select all.
  1=Select

Opt          Query Definition Option
 _         > Specify file selections
 _           Define result fields
 _           Select and sequence fields
 _           Select records
 _           Select sort fields
 _           Select collating sequence
 _           Specify report column formatting
 _           Select report summary functions
 _           Define report breaks
 _           Select output type and output form
 _           Specify processing options

F3=Exit          F5=Report                F12=Cancel
F13=Layout       F18=Files                F21=Select all
Select options, or press F3 to save or run the query.
```

Figure 4.2
Select Sort Fields Screen

```
                              Select Sort Fields

Type sort priority (0-999) and A (Ascending) or D (Descending) for the names of up
  to 32 fields, press Enter.

Sort
Prty A/D     Field          Text                            Len      Dec
 ___  _      EMPID          EMP ID                            4
 ___  _      DEPTNO         DEPT NO                           3
 ___  _      NAME           EMPLOYEE NAME                    20
 ___  _      MONSAL         MONTHLY SALARY                    6        2

                                                                      Bottom
F3=Exit        F5=Report      F11=Display       F12=Cancel
F13=Layout     F18=Files      F20=Renumber      F24=More keys
```

sort field, and it would be assigned a higher number. The numbers may be any one- to three-digit number. Therefore, the state field could be assigned a one, and the city field assigned a two; or the state field could be assigned a 10, and the city field assigned a 20.

You have two choices for sequencing each field that will be sorted, ascending or descending. The ascending sort places fields in alphabetical sequence, A to Z, while the descending sort places fields in sequence Z to A. Numeric fields sorted in ascending order are in order of increasing numeric value, while those sorted in descending order are in order of decreasing numeric value.

This chapter exercise will have the department number as the major sort field and the employee name as the minor sort field. Both fields will be sorted in ascending sequence.

TIP: If your screen does not show the field information (column heading, length, and decimals), you will need to press F11 to display this data.

Press	**Tab** twice	to bypass the EMP ID line
Type	**1**	in Sort Prty column before DEPTNO
Press	**Field Exit**	
Type	**A**	in Ascending/Descending for DEPTNO
Type	**2**	in Sort Prty column before NAME
Press	**Field Exit**	
Type	**A**	in Ascending/Descending for NAME
Press	**Enter**	

See Figure 4.3 for a screen display representing these actions.

Figure 4.3
Select Sort Fields Screen

```
                         Select Sort Fields

Type sort priority (0-999) and A (Ascending) or D (Descending) for the names of up
  to 32 fields, press Enter.

Sort
Prty A/D    Field         Text                          Len    Dec
   1  A     DEPTNO        DEPT NO                         3
   2  A     NAME          EMPLOYEE NAME                  20
 ___  _     EMPID         EMP ID                          4
 ___  _     MONSAL        MONTHLY SALARY                  6      2








                                                                      Bottom
F3-Exit          F5-Report          F11-Display          F12-Cancel
F13-Layout       F18-Files          F20-Renumber         F24-More keys
Press Enter to confirm.
```

Notice the message at the bottom of the screen.

Press	**Enter**	to confirm the sort selection
Press	**F5**	to display the report

Compare Figure 4.4 to your output for accuracy.

Figure 4.4
Display Report Screen

```
                              Display Report
                                                        Report width . . .53
Position to line . . . ______ Shift to column  . . . . . .__
Line   ....+....1....+....2....+....3....+....4....+....5...
       DEPT NO  EMPLOYEE NAME         EMP ID  MONTHLY SALARY
000001   100    ADAMS, MARK           2567         1,546.50
000002   100    POWERS, SUSAN         6340         1,725.00
000003   200    GREEN, TOM            5632         1,200.00
000004   300    HART, BOB             5718         1,222.00
000005   400    JONES, BILL           1234         1,322.00
000006   400    KLEIN, JOHN           7290         1,400.00
000007   400    WALKER, GARY          0516         1,775.25
000008   500    TUCKER, MARY          1892         1,500.00
000009   600    BLACKBERG, KAREN      4672         1,300.00
000010   600    SMITHE, CAROL         3567         1,567.75
****** ********  End of report  *******

                                                                  Bottom
F3=Exit     F12=Cancel     F19=Left     F20=Right     F21=Split
```

The Query report has been generated in the requested sequence, alphabetic employee name within department number.

Press	**F12**	to clear the display when you have compared your display to the text
Press	**F3**	to access the save and exit screen
Press	**Tab**	to bypass the "Y"
Type	**2**	as the Run Option
Type	**paymstq4**	as the query save name
Press	**Field Exit**	
Press	**Tab**	to bypass the library
Type	**PAYMST Query by name within dept sequence**	as the Text information
Press	**Enter**	to save and run the Query report

The Query report will be on your output queue with the name QPQUPRFIL.

Review Questions

1. Explain the purpose of the Select sort fields option.
2. Is the input file resequenced by using this Select sort fields option?

Exercises

1. Create a Query report that will sequence the DPTMST file into department number order. Print all fields with the department number first. Save this report as CH4EX1.
2. Create a Query report that will sequence the DPTMST file into department name order. Print all fields with the department name first. Save this report as CH4EX2.
3. Create a Query report that will sequence the ADRMST file into alphabetic order by city name. Print all fields with the city as the left-most field. Save this report as CH4EX3.
4. Create a Query report that will sequence the ADRMST file into descending zip code sequence. Print all fields with the zip code as the first field. Save this report as CH4EX4.

Chapter 5

Selecting Records for Reporting

Objectives:

- ✓ To understand Query's logical conditions
- ✓ To understand how to select one or more records from the input file based on one or more logical conditions

Introduction

This chapter describes how to choose records from the input file(s) when generating a Query report so that your output is only a portion of the input file. Production databases usually have a large number of records, and rarely does a user require all the records on any one report. This chapter exercise will be to refine the Query from Chapter 3, and to eliminate employees who are not eligible for the 5 percent raise. Any employee who earns less than $1,300 per month will not be eligible for the raise. Both the employee's current salary and the proposed increased salary need to be displayed to provide management with adequate information. The user has also requested that the employee ID not be shown on the report, and that the report must be in the sequence of employee name within department number.

You will generate this report through a series of refinements to the Query definition, PAYMSTQ3, that was created in Chapter 3. You will save a new Query definition, PAYMSTQ5. You will not actually change file PAYMSTQ3, but will use it only as the basis for a new definition. This saves time because you already know that the raise has been correctly calculated in PAYMSTQ3.

Let's begin by accessing the Work with Queries menu.

Type	**WRKQRY**	on any command line
Press	**Enter**	

Figure 5.1 shows the Work with Queries menu.

To change a query, use the Change function, and enter the name of the query to be changed.

Figure 5.1
Work with Queries Menu

```
                              Work with Queries

Type choices, press Enter.

  Option . . . . _          1=Create, 2=Change, 3=Copy,4=Delete
                            5=Display, 6=Print definition
                            8=Run in batch, 9=Run
  Query  . . . . __________ Name, F4 for list
    Library. . .   yourname Name, *LIBL, F4 for list









F3=Exit        F4=Prompt        F5=Refresh        F12=Cancel
```

Type	**2**	to change an existing query
Type	**paymstq3**	as the query to change
Press	**Enter**	
Press	**F5**	to run your paymstq3 query

See Figure 5.2 to be certain you have the correct query from Chapter 3. If your report does not match, reference Chapter 3 to determine your error.

Figure 5.2
Display Report Screen Showing PAYMSTQ3 Query

```
                              Display Report
                                                         Report width . . .65
Position to line . . . _____         Shift to column  . . . . . . __
Line     ....+....1....+....2....+....3....+....4....+....5....+..
         EMP ID  DEPT NO  EMPLOYEE NAME   MONTHLY SALARY NEW SALARY
000001    1234     400    JONES, BILL          1,322.00    1,388.10
000002    3567     600    SMITHE, CAROL        1,567.75    1,646.14
000003    5632     200    GREEN, TOM           1,200.00    1,260.00
000004    2567     100    ADAMS, MARK          1,546.50    1,623.83
000005    4672     600    BLACKBERG, KAREN     1,300.00    1,365.00
000006    7290     400    KLEIN, JOHN          1,400.00    1,470.00
000007    1892     500    TUCKER, MARY         1,500.00    1,575.00
000008    0516     400    WALKER, GARY         1,775.25    1,864.01
000009    6340     100    POWERS, SUSAN        1,725.00    1,811.25
000010    5718     300    HART, BOB            1,222.00    1,283.10
******   ********  End of report  ******



                                                                     Bottom
F3=Exit     F12=Cancel     F19=Left     F20=Right        F21=Split
```

Press	**F12**	after you have verified the report
Type	**1**	to Select records
Press	**Enter**	

This report requires that an employee's monthly salary be $1,300 or more before the 5 percent raise is calculated. Because PAYMSTQ3 has the new salary already calculated, this chapter is only concerned with selecting the correct group of employees to receive the raise.

The Select records screen is shown in Figure 5.3.

Figure 5.3
Select Records Screen

```
                                Select Records

Type comparisons, press Enter.  Specify OR to start each new group.  Tests:  EQ, NE,
LE, GE, LT, GT, RANGE, LIST, LIKE..

AND/OR      Field      Test          Value (Field, Number, 'Char'...)
            _____      ____          ________________________________
_______     _____      ____          ________________________________
_______     _____      ____          ________________________________
_______     _____      ____          ________________________________
_______     _____      ____          ________________________________
                                                                          Bottom
....................................................................................
Field       Column Heading                                 Len     Dec
EMPID       EMP ID                                           4
DEPTNO      DEPT NO                                          3
NAME        EMPLOYEE NAME                                   20
MONSAL      MONTHLY SALARY                                   6       2
NEWSAL      MONSAL*1.05                                      6       2

                                                                          Bottom
F3=Exit        F5=Report      F9=Insert         F11=Display names
F12=Cancel     F13=Layout     F20=Reorganize    F24=More keys
```

Figure 5.3 shows that Query has split the screen into two parts. The top portion is for defining the comparison information: the field name, the comparison test, and the value(s) to be used for the test.

TIP: You can specify a maximum of 100 comparisons. Use the Shift/Roll Up keys to get more blank input lines.

TIP: If your screen does not show the field information (column heading, length, and decimals), press **F11** to display this data.

The lower portion of the screen contains a list of the existing field names. This is for your convenience so you do not have to remember which fields are within the input record or are newly defined, or how the field names are spelled.

TIP: If more fields are available than can be seen (More...), move your cursor to the lower half of the screen and use the Shift/Roll Up keys to look at all the fields.

Comparison Tests

You can compare fields to each other and to numeric or character constants using the following tests:

EQ	Equal
NE	Not equal
LT	Less than
GT	Greater than
LE	Less than or equal
GE	Greater than or equal

You can compare fields to numeric or character constants with the following tests:

LIKE	Does the content of a field have a pattern similar to the value?
LIST	Is the content of a field equal to one of the values in the list?
RANGE	Is the content of a field within a range of values?

A numeric constant can be up to 31 digits long. Numeric constants may include a decimal point, but no dollar signs or commas. A character constant may be any combination of alphanumeric characters, enclosed in apostrophes; for example, 'SMITH'. If you do not enclose a character constant in apostrophes, Query assumes that the group of characters is a field name. Query is also case sensitive, so you must type uppercase and lowercase to get the exact match.

Consider the example of selecting all the customers who have the title of "Ms" in the title field of the database. The Field would be Title, the Test would be equal, and the Value would be 'Ms'. The Select records entry would be `TITLE EQ 'Ms'`.

Consider the request that a report be generated for all employees who have been with the company more than 15 years. Assuming that 15 years ago was 1977, with a Field of Hireyr, the Test would be less than or equal, and the Value would be 1977. The Select records entry would be `HIREYR LE 1977`.

You could compare a reorder field in an inventory system with the inventory on hand. If the reorder field was greater than or equal to the inventory on hand, this record would be selected for printing so that more inventory could be purchased. In this example, the Field would be reorder and the Test would be greater than or equal to the second field of inventory on hand, `REORDER GE ONHAND`.

If you needed a report of all the employees with the last name of Smith you could compare the last name field for an equal on 'SMITH ' or 'Smith ', if you were not sure whether uppercase or a combination of uppercase and lowercase had been used. The Select records entry would be `LNAME LIST 'SMITH ' 'Smith '`. A space must be included as the last character within the quotes if you do not want to include names such as Smithsonian.

There are times when it is convenient to be able to select a range of values. For example, let's say there are 15 marketing regions. To hold a marketing seminar for the Midwest regions, you need to print labels for the regions from 3 to 7. Regions 1, 2, and 8 through 15 are to be excluded. The Field would be region, the Test would be the word Range, and the value would be entered as 3 7. The values for the range must be separated by a space. The Select records entry would be `REGION RANGE 3 7`. The range values are inclusive.

You can use the LIKE comparison only on character fields. This test is used to select a record if a certain part of the field has the same character(s) as the pattern that you specify in the value. You would use the underscore (_) to skip one character in a particular position, and the percent sign (%) to skip one or more characters. For example, you would use the LIKE test to select all of the employees whose last name is SMITH, assuming the name field contained both last and first name. The Value would be 'SMITH %'. The Select records entry would be `NAME LIKE 'SMITH %'`. If the field separated last name from first name with a comma, the entry would be `NAME LIKE 'SMITH,%'`.

To select everyone who lives on Main Street would be another use of the LIKE comparison. The house number may vary in length and the street designation may or may not be present, therefore % would be used at each end of Main. The Select records entry would be `STREET LIKE '% Main %'`.

Figure 5.4 shows how the above examples would be keyed on a Select records screen. This figure is for illustrative purposes only. These examples are not all part of the same selection.

Figure 5.4
Select Records Screen Example Comparisons

AND/OR	Field	Test	Value (Field, Number, 'Char'...)
_	TITLE	EQ	'Ms'
_	HIREYR	LE	1977
_	REORDER	GE	ONHAND
_	LNAME	LIST	'SMITH ' 'Smith '
_	REGION	RANGE	3 7
_	NAME	LIKE	'SMITH %'
_	NAME	LIKE	'SMITH,%'
_	STREET	LIKE	'% Main %'

Using AND/OR Comparisons

To use more than one comparison to select a record, you must connect the comparisons with an AND or an OR. AND will be interpreted that both of the comparisons must be true before a record will be selected. OR will be interpreted that only one of the comparisons must be true for a record to be selected. A combination of AND and OR can be used for a complex comparison. However, using both AND and OR may be logically confusing, and you should avoid doing so unless you are a programming expert.

One Select records screen is used to make the record selections from a file. If you key in multiple selections and leave the first column blank, Query assumes the selections are connected with AND.

An AND example would be to select only the employees from department number 400 who have a salary greater than $20,000:

AND/OR	Field	Test	Value (Field, Number, 'Char'...)
	DEPTNO	EQ	'400'
AND	MONSAL	GT	20000

Another AND example would be to select all female employees who make more than $25,000 and were born before 1950:

AND/OR	Field	Test	Value (Field, Number, 'Char'...)
	GENDER	EQ	'F'
AND	MONSAL	GT	25000
AND	BDATE	LT	1950

An OR example would be to select any employee from department 400 or any employee who has a salary greater than $20,000.

AND/OR	Field	Test	Value (Field, Number, 'Char'...)
	DPTNO	EQ	'400'
OR	MONSAL	GT	20000

Another OR example would be to select any student who has a grade point average of 3.5 and above, or any student who received an "A" in the advanced calculus course.

AND/OR	Field	Test	Value (Field, Number, 'Char'...)
	GPA	GE	3.5
OR	CRSNME	EQ	'ADVANCED CALCULUS'

Completing the Chapter Record Selection

Continue working on the chapter Query report. For an employee to be listed on the report, he or she must have an existing salary of $1,300 per month or more. The correct entries are shown in Figure 5.5.

Type	**MONSAL**	as the field name
Press	**Field Exit**	
Type	**GE**	as the test
Press	**Field Exit**	
Type	**1300**	as the value

Press	**Enter**	when your entries are correct
Press	**F5**	to run the report

Figure 5.5
Select Records Screen

```
                              Select Records

Type comparisons, press Enter.  Specify OR to start each new group.  Tests:  EQ, NE,
LE, GE, LT, GT, RANGE, LIST, LIKE..

AND/OR     Field     Test     Value (Field, Number, 'Char'...)
           MONSAL    GE       1300
___        ______    _____    ________________________________
___        ______    _____    ________________________________
___        ______    _____    ________________________________
___        ______    _____    ________________________________
___        ______    _____    ________________________________
                                                                      Bottom
..................................................................................
Field      Column Heading                                 Len      Dec
EMPID      EMP ID                                           4
DEPTNO     DEPT NO                                          3
NAME       EMPLOYEE NAME                                   20
MONSAL     MONTHLY SALARY                                   6        2
NEWSAL     MONSAL*1.05                                      6        2
                                                                      Bottom
F3-Exit        F5-Report      F9-Insert          F11-Display names
F12-Cancel     F13-Layout     F20-Reorganize     F24-More keys
```

Compare your screen to the report shown in Figure 5.6 for accuracy.

Figure 5.6
Display Report Screen

```
                              Display Report
                                                        Report width . . .65
Position to line . . . _____          Shift to column  . . . . . .__
Line       ....+....1....+....2....+....3....+....4....+....5....+..
           EMP ID  DEPT NO  EMPLOYEE NAME     MONTHLY SALARY   NEW SAL
000001      1234     400    JONES, BILL           1,322.00    1,388.10
000002      3567     600    SMITHE, CAROL         1,567.75    1,646.14
000003      2567     100    ADAMS, MARK           1,546.50    1,623.83
000004      4672     600    BLACKBERG, KAREN      1,300.00    1,365.00
000005      7290     400    KLEIN, JOHN           1,400.00    1,470.00
000006      1892     500    TUCKER, MARY          1,500.00    1,575.00
000007      0516     400    WALKER, GARY          1,775.25    1,864.01
000008      6430     100    POWERS, SUSAN         1,725.00    1,811.25
******     ********     End of report     ******

                                                                      Bottom
F3-Exit      F12-Cancel      F19-Left      F20-Right        F21-Split
```

Notice that the report has dropped from 10 records to eight records. This Query report has selected to display only those employees whose monthly salary is greater than $1,300. However, there were other specifications for this report. Management does not want the employee ID to print, and the report is supposed to print in department order, with employees listed alphabetically within each department. Therefore, you need to make more report selections.

Press	**F12**	to clear the display
Type	**1**	to choose the Select and sequence fields option to make a change
Press	**Enter**	
Type		the correct entry(ies) to eliminate the employee ID, as shown in previous chapters
Press	**Enter twice**	to confirm the selection
Type	**1**	to choose the Select sort fields option
Press	**Enter**	
Type		the correct entry(ies) to sort the employees alphabetically within department
Press	**Enter twice**	to confirm the sort fields
Press	**F5**	to display the report shown in Figure 5.7

Figure 5.7
Display Report Menu

```
                                Display Report
                                                           Report width . . .60
Position to line . . .                 Shift to column  . . . . . .
Line      ....+....1....+....2....+....3....+....4....+....5....+..
          DEPT NO  EMPLOYEE NAME      MONTHLY SALARY     NEW SALARY
000001     100     ADAMS, MARK            1,546.50         1,623.83
000002     100     POWERS, SUSAN          1,725.00         1,811.25
000003     400     JONES, BILL            1,322.00         1,388.10
000004     400     KLEIN, JOHN            1,400.00         1,470.00
000005     400     WALKER, GARY           1,775.25         1,864.01
000006     500     TUCKER, MARY           1,500.00         1,575.00
000007     600     BLACKBERG, KAREN       1,300.00         1,365.00
000008     600     SMITHE, CAROL          1,567.75         1,646.14
******  ********    End of report    ******



                                                                         Bottom
F3=Exit       F12=Cancel       F19=Left       F20=Right          F21=Split
```

Compare your output to Figure 5.7 for accuracy. Clear the report from the screen and save the query with the name PAYMSTQ5.

Press	**F12**	to clear the report
Press	**F3**	to the save the Query

See Figure 5.8 for the Exit this Query menu.

Press	**Tab** twice	to bypass save definition and run option
Type	**PAYMSTQ5**	as the query name, over the old name, PAYMSTQ3
Type	**PAYMST in sequence with selected records**	as the text, over the old text
Press	**Enter**	

Figure 5.8
Exit this Query Screen

```
                              Exit this Query

Type choices, press Enter.

  Save definition . . . . .   Y              Y-Yes, N-No

  Run Option  . . . . . . .   2              1-Run interactively
                                             2-Run in Batch
                                             3-Do not run

  For a saved definition:
    Query . . . . . . . . .   PAYMSTQ3       Name
      Library . . . . . . .   yourname       Name, F4 for list

    Text  . . . . . . . . .   PAYMST Query with result field

  Authority . . . . . . . .   *CHANGE        *LIBCRTAUT, *CHANGE,
                                             *ALL, *EXCLUDE,
                                             *USE, authorized
                                             list name

F4-Prompt          F5-Report          F12-Cancel      F13-Layout
F14-Define the query
```

The PAYMSTQ3 file has not been changed. You have used it as the basis for a new query, PAYMSTQ5.

Review Questions

1. Explain the purpose of the Select Records option.
2. What type of fields may be compared to the value field?
3. What operators may be used with a numeric field?
4. What is the purpose of the RANGE expression?
5. When should single quotes be used within the value area?

Exercises

1. Use the PAYMST file and create a report for all employees who make less than $1,300 a month, giving each a 6.5 percent raise (format as a length of 6 with 2 decimals). Print all the fields from PAYMST, the new RAISE field, and the new salary amount (MONSAL + RAISE). Save this report as CH5EX1.
2. Use the DPTMST file and print a report with all the DPTMST fields for departments with budgets between $51,000 and $125,000. Save this report as CH5EX2.
3. Use the ADRMST file and select all the phone numbers with an area code of 615 and lower. Print phone number and street address. Save this report as CH5EX3.
4. Use the PAYMST file. Sort by employee name within department. Print employee name and department for employees in departments 200 through 600. Save this report as CH5EX4.
5. Use the PAYMST file. Select employees with salaries greater than $1,500. Print all fields for employees, in alphabetical sequence by employee name. Save this report as CH5EX5.
6. Use the PAYMSTQ3 file from Chapter 3. Print a report that includes only employees from departments 100 and 600 who have a NEWSAL greater than $1,600. Print only employee name, salary, and new salary, and print the report in employee name sequence. Save the report as CH5EX6.
7. Use the PAYMST file. Print all fields for employees whose employee ID contains a one (1) as the leading digit of the ID number. Save the report as CH5EX7.

Chapter 6

Using Summary Functions

Objectives:

- ✓ To understand how to use the Query summary functions
- ✓ To understand the EBCDIC collating sequence

Introduction

This chapter describes how to use the Query summary functions for any field in a Query definition. Report requests frequently include mathematical calculations for counting the number of items selected, totaling a column of values, or calculating averages, minimums, and maximums. You can specify all these summary calculations for numeric fields. Character fields may use count, minimum, and maximum.

Selecting the Report Summary Functions

A request has been made to count the number of employees who may be eligible for a 5 percent raise, to sum the total dollars of the current salary, and to sum the total dollars for the proposed salary increase. You will use the Query definition from Chapter 5, PAYMSTQ5, as the basis for PAYMSTQ6. Work with Query and use the Change function for PAYMSTQ5.

Press	**F5**	to run your paymstq5 query

See Figure 6.1 to be certain you have the correct query from Chapter 5. If your report does not match, reference Chapter 5 to determine your error.

Press	**F12**	after you have checked your PAYMSTQ5 query
Type	**1**	in the option column to Select report summary functions
Press	**Enter**	

Figure 6.1
Display Report Screen Showing PAYMSTQ5 Query

```
                                  Display Report
                                                              Report width . . .60
Position to line . . . ______     Shift to column  . . . . . ._
Line      ....+....1....+....2....+....3....+....4....+....5....+..
          DEPT NO  EMPLOYEE NAME       MONTHLY SALARY    NEW SALARY
000001     100     ADAMS, MARK              1,546.50       1,623.83
000002     100     POWERS, SUSAN            1,725.00       1,811.25
000003     400     JONES, BILL              1,322.00       1,388.10
000004     400     KLEIN, JOHN              1,400.00       1,470.00
000005     400     WALKER, GARY             1,775.25       1,864.01
000006     500     TUCKER, MARY             1,500.00       1,575.00
000007     600     BLACKBERG, KAREN         1,300.00       1,365.00
000008     600     SMITHE, CAROL            1,567.75       1,646.14
******  ********   End of report  ******

                                                                        Bottom
F3-Exit    F12-Cancel    F19-Left    F20-Right        F21-Split
```

See Figure 6.2 for an example of the report summary functions display.

Figure 6.2
Select Report Summary Functions Screen

```
                        Select Report Summary Functions

Type options, press Enter.
  1-Total    2-Average    3-Minimum    4-Maximum    5-Count

---Options---          Field      Text                      Len      Dec
_  _  _  _  _          DEPTNO     DEPT NO                     3
_  _  _  _  _          NAME       EMPLOYEE NAME              20
_  _  _  _  _          MONSAL     MONTHLY SALARY              6        2
_  _  _  _  _          NEWSAL     MONSAL*1.05                 6        2

                                                                        Bottom
F3-Exit        F5-Report      F10-Process     F11-Display names
F12-Cancel     F13-Layout     F18-Files       F23-Long comment
```

The Select Report Summary Functions option allows the five different types of calculations shown on the option line. Each field may use none or all five calculations, depending on whether the field is numeric or character, and the user's requirements. The Total option sums the contents of any numeric field. A total could be for the entire report, or for a group of records in a report break (see Chapter 7).

The Average function calculates the average of a numeric field based on the number of records in the group being averaged. An average could be for the entire report, or for a group of records in a report break (see Chapter 7).

The Count function will tally the number of records selected for either a report break or the entire report. Count differs from Total in that the contents of the field are not summed; each record counted is tallied as one item. Therefore, Count may be used on either numeric or character fields.

Minimum and Maximum will locate the lowest or highest number or character. The AS/400 is an EBCDIC computer and sequences character fields in the order shown in Figure 6.3. For example, Smith would compare lower than SMITH and Smith would compare lower than SABLE. Remember that a space is a character, and that spaces in a field will always be lower than any other character. See Appendix B for more information about collating sequences.

Figure 6.3
EBCDIC Collating Sequence Summary

EBCDIC Collating Sequence Summary

blanks	low
special characters	.
lowercase, a to z	.
uppercase, A to Z	.
0 to 9	high

To continue the chapter exercise,

Press	**Tab**	to bypass options for Deptno
Type	**5**	in the options column before the Name field, to count the number of selected records
Press	**Tab**	to bypass the remaining options for Name
Type	**1**	in the options column before the Monthly Salary, to total Monthly Salary
Press	**Tab**	to bypass the remaining options for Monthly Salary
Type	**1**	in the options column before the New Salary, to total New Salary
Press	**Enter**	
Press	**F5**	

Compare your display to Figure 6.4 for accuracy.

Figure 6.4
Display Report Screen

```
                              Display Report
                                                              Report width . . .60
Position to line . . . ______       Shift to column  . . . . . ._
Line    ....+....1....+....2....+....3....+....4....+....5....+..6
       DEPT NO  EMPLOYEE NAME               MONTHLY SALARY   NEW SALARY
000001   100    ADAMS, MARK                    1,546.50       1,623.83
000002   100    POWERS, SUSAN                  1,725.00       1,811.25
000003   400    JONES, BILL                    1,322.00       1,388.10
000004   400    KLEIN, JOHN                    1,400.00       1,470.00
000005   400    WALKER, GARY                   1,775.25       1,864.01
000006   500    TUCKER, MARY                   1,500.00       1,575.00
000007   600    BLACKBERG, KAREN               1,300.00       1,365.00
000008   600    SMITHE, CAROL                  1,567.75       1,646.14
000009
000010      FINAL TOTALS
000011      TOTAL                             12,136.50      12,743.33
000012      COUNT 8
****** ********  End of report  ********

                                                                  Bottom
F3=Exit      F12=Cancel      F19=Left      F20=Right          F21=Split
```

A field's totals are printed in the same column as the field and have the same number of decimal places. Figure 6.4 shows the Count function's value displayed next to the word COUNT. Note that eight records were selected.

Press	**F12**	to clear the report
Press	**F3**	to save the Query as PAYMSTQ6, with an appropriate text description

Review Questions

1. Explain the difference between the Report Summary functions COUNT and TOTAL.
2. Using the EBCDIC Collating Sequence Summary from Figure 6.3, determine what would be the minimum and maximum values from each of the following two lists of field values.

List 1 - Numeric

547321	015632
087256	014665
014660	014666
876320	876300
111110	087554

List 2 - Character

JONES	JUSTIN
Jack	Jason
JASON	Jeff
Justin	jump
JEFF	JUMP
JACK	jazz
Jones	Jazz

Exercises

1. Print the average, maximum, and minimum monthly and new salaries using the query created in this chapter, PAYMSTQ6, as the basis. Do not print a TOTAL or COUNT. Save the report as CH6EX1.
2. Print all the Oregon addresses from the ADRMST file, and count the number of records. Save the report as CH6EX2.
3. Use the DPTMST file. Print only the department name and annual budget fields from each record. Print the total, average, maximum, and minimum annual budget amounts. Save the report as CH6EX3.

Chapter 7

Using Report Breaks

Objectives:

- ✓ To understand the purpose of a report break
- ✓ To be able to define multiple report breaks
- ✓ To be able to use variables with report break text

Introduction

Report breaks, often called control breaks, are a method of providing subtotals and/or page breaks for reports that are in sequence by one or more fields. These report breaks may be as simple as listing an address file in state sequence or printing the number of addresses within each state. Another example is a personnel file that must be sequenced to print all the female employees and a count, followed by all the male employees and a count. Or the personnel file could be printed with each department as a group, with corresponding counts and salary summaries.

Report breaks may also be quite complex, depending on the data. Consider an international company that conducts business in six countries. The board of directors requires information on the total corporation's activities and also needs to compare sales by country. The CEO of each country is interested only in the sales figures for his/her particular country. Regional managers want totals for their respective regions and data on how each state was performing. Managers at the state level are interested in reports about the performance of each marketing representative. Query reports can break the corporate marketing data into these six levels of information. See Figure 7.1 for a partial Query report with six control breaks.

Query will generate information with all the supporting detail lines, or you can select summary reports for upper-level managers who wish to see only the totals. A detail report prints a line for every record selected to be in the report. A summary report prints only the summaries of groups of detail information. See Chapter 10 for instructions to print summary reports.

Figure 7.1
Partial Query Report with Six Control Breaks

```
Country  USA
     Region  East Coast
          State  Connecticut
               County  Fairfield
                    City  New Haven
                         Sales Repr Alice
                              Sale 1
                              Sale 2
                              Sale 3
                         Total Sales for Repr Alice          $99,999.99
                         Sales Repr Bob
                              Sale 1
                              Sale 2
                              Sale 3
                         Total Sales for Repr Bob            $99,999.99
                    City  New Haven Total Sales             $999,999.99

                    City  Stanford
                         Sales Repr Alice
                              Sale 1
                              Sale 2
                              Sale 3
                         Total Sales for Repr Alice          $99,999.99
                         Sales Repr Bob
                              Sale 1
                              Sale 2
                              Sale 3
                         Total Sales for Repr Bob            $99,999.99
                    City  Stanford Total Sales              $999,999.99
```

Report Break Information

Report breaks separate a report into groups when there is a change in the value of a report break field. The input file must be in this report break field sequence for the program to work correctly. Therefore, you must use Query's Select sort fields option to make this option work correctly. You will use the Define report breaks option to control the report break information. And you use the Select report summary functions option to designate which fields for a break will be counted, summed, averaged, and so on.

Break level is the Query term for establishing the hierarchy of a report break report. Up to six break levels can be defined, numbered 1 through 6. A break level of 1 has a higher priority than a break level of 6. In the international company example from Figure 7.1, country would be level 1, region would be level 2, state would be level 3, county would be level 4, city would be level 5, and sales representative would be level 6.

Break level 0 is the final total break. Final totals are printed at the end of the report. Summary report functions and page breaks are automatically processed when there is a change in the requested break field value.

Any field can be used as the report break field, but the field should contain several of the same values. It would not make sense to use a name field as the controlling field because most people's names are different. If a break were defined on a name field, Query would generate a report break after every name that has a different spelling.

Defining Report Breaks

In the Query report that you have been developing throughout the previous chapters, each department head may need to know the effect of the pay raise on his/her budget. Report breaks at the end of the list of each department's employees would be helpful. This chapter will develop a report break for each department. The output of Chapter 6, file PAYMSTQ6, will be used as the basis for file PAYMSTQ7. Begin Query and use the Change function for file PAYMSTQ6.

Press	**F5**	to run your PAYMSTQ6 query

See Figure 7.2 to be certain you have the correct query from Chapter 6.

Figure 7.2
Display Report Screen Showing PAYMSTQ6 Query

```
                                    Display Report
                                                                 Report width . . .60
Position to line . . . ______        Shift to column  . . . . . .__
Line    ....+....1....+....2....+....3....+....4....+....5....+..6
          DEPT NO   EMPLOYEE NAME                MONTHLY SALARY   NEW SALARY
000001     100      ADAMS, MARK                     1,546.50        1,623.83
000002     100      POWERS, SUSAN                   1,725.00        1,811.25
000003     400      JONES, BILL                     1,322.00        1,388.10
000004     400      KLEIN, JOHN                     1,400.00        1,470.00
000005     400      WALKER, GARY                    1,775.25        1,864.01
000006     500      TUCKER, MARY                    1,500.00        1,575.00
000007     600      BLACKBERG, KAREN                1,300.00        1,365.00
000008     600      SMITHE, CAROL                   1,567.75        1,646.14
000009
000010       FINAL TOTALS
000011       TOTAL                                 12,136.50       12,743.33
000012       COUNT 8
****** ********    End of report   ********

                                                                          Bottom
F3=Exit      F12=Cancel      F19=Left      F20=Right          F21=Split
```

If your report does not match, reference Chapter 6 to determine your error.

Press	**F12**	after you have checked your PAYMSTQ6 query
Type	**1**	to Define report breaks
Press	**Enter**	

See Figure 7.3 for the Define Report Breaks screen.

Figure 7.3
Define Report Breaks Screen

```
                              Define Report Breaks

Type break level(1-6) for up to 9 field names, press Enter.
    (Use as many fields as needed for each break level.)

Break     Sort
Level     Prty        Field      Text                      Len  Dec
  _       10          DEPTNO     DEPT NO                     3
  _       20          NAME       EMPLOYEE NAME              20
  _                   MONSAL     MONTHLY SALARY              6    2
  _                   NEWSAL     MONSAL*1.05                 6    2

                                                                   Bottom
F3-Exit        F5-Report      F10-Process    F11-Display names
F12-Cancel     F13-Layout     F18-Files      F23-Long comment
```

Each field defined for a report break *must* have been previously selected as a sort field. Notice that fields DEPTNO and NAME are displayed on the screen with an entry in the Sort Priority column. Department number will be the only break field. Remember that name would rarely be used as a break field, because it contains unique data.

Type **1** in the level break column for DEPTNO
Press **Enter**

You will now see Figure 7.4 displayed on your screen, the Format Report Break menu for break level 0. Break level 0 is for the final totals. When you select this break level, Query assumes you want something printed at the end of a report.

Figure 7.4
Format Report Break Screen

```
                              Format Report Break

Break level . . . . . . . . : 0

Type choices, press Enter.
  (Type &field in text to have break values inserted.)

  Suppress summaries  . . . : N                Y-Yes, N-No

  Break text  . . . . . . . : FINAL TOTALS


Level   Field
  1     DEPTNO


F3-Exit        F5-Report      F10-Process         F12-Cancel
F13-Layout     F18-Files      F23-Long comment
```

Query generates final totals automatically whenever the Query option Select report summary functions has been defined. Final totals will automatically be printed with text of "FINAL TOTALS" unless the Suppress summaries option is changed to "Yes". You can suppress summary level printing at any break level. If you are going to print the final totals, you can define the text printed with the totals. You can enter a maximum of 40 characters for this break text.

For the chapter exercise, you will keep the final totals and change the final break text.

Press	**Tab**	to bypass the Suppress summaries option
Type	**End of Report Totals**	in place of the Break text FINAL TOTALS
Press	**Enter**	

Another Format Report Break screen, Figure 7.5, appears for each break level you have defined. You defined only one break level, department number. Therefore, this screen's information will print at the end of a group of employees who have the same department number. If you had defined more than one break level, you would answer the same questions for each break level.

Figure 7.5
Format Report Break Screen

```
                          Format Report Break

Break level . . . . . . . . . : 1

Type choices, press Enter.
  (Type &field in text to have break values inserted.)

  Skip to new page  . . . . . : N                Y=Yes, N=No

  Suppress summaries  . . . . : N                Y=Yes, N=No

  Break text  . . . . . . . . : ________________________________

Level  Field
  1    DEPTNO




F3=Exit        F5=Report      F10=Process             F12=Cancel
F13=Layout     F18=Files      F23=Long comment
```

Three options are available for a report break. After each break for a control field is printed, you might choose to skip to a new page. If you need to tear the report apart to provide it to individual departments, change the Skip to a new page option from N to Y. Change the Suppress summaries option from N to Y if you do not want the summaries (total, average, minimum, maximum, and/or count) printed.

The break text printed at the end of each group can contain a maximum of 40 characters. Because this break is by department, you might want to enter the text "DEPARTMENT TOTALS" to print when the subtotals print. The break text may also have data values printed in it; for example, the actual department number for the previous detail lines. This is very helpful when there are many pages for a particular group. To print a value of a variable, enter the field name for the data value, proceeded by an ampersand (&). The allowable break field names to use for this option are always displayed on the lower portion of the screen.

TIP: Suppressed summaries do not stop the break text from printing. Break text should also be deleted when summaries are suppressed.

The break text for the chapter exercise should be printed as "Department xxx Totals," where xxx is the department number. Use the following instructions:

Press	**Tab**	to bypass the skip to a new page option
Press	**Tab**	to bypass the suppress summaries
Type	**Department &DEPTNO Totals**	as the break text
Press	**Enter**	
Press	**F5**	to run the report

The report breaks are now completed. See Figures 7.6 and 7.7 to verify your work.

TIP: The report cannot be displayed on one screen. Use the Shift/Roll Up keys to view the entire report.

Figure 7.6
Display Report Screen, Screen 1

```
                                  Display Report
                                                           Report width . . .60
Position to line . . .               Shift to column  . . . . . .
Line     ....+....1....+....2....+....3....+....4....+....5....+..6
         DEPT NO  EMPLOYEE NAME         MONTHLY SALARY   NEW SALARY
000001   100      ADAMS, MARK              1,546.50        1,623.83
000002   100      POWERS, SUSAN            1,725.00        1,811.25
000003
000004      Department 100 Totals
000005      TOTAL                          3,271.50        3,435.08
000006      COUNT 2
000007
000008   400      JONES, BILL              1,322.00        1,388.10
000009   400      KLEIN, JOHN              1,400.00        1,470.00
000010   400      WALKER, GARY             1,775.25        1,864.01
000011
000012     Department 400 Totals
000013     TOTAL                           4,497.25        4,722.11
000014     COUNT 3
000015
000016   500      TUCKER, MARY             1,500.00        1,575.00
                                                                     More...

F3-Exit      F12-Cancel      F19-Left      F20-Right        F21-Split
```

Figure 7.7
Display Report Screen, Screen 2

```
                                 Display Report
                                                                    Report width . . .60
Position to line . . . ______   Shift to column . . . . . . __
Line    ....+....1....+....2....+....3....+....4....+....5....+..6
        DEPT NO  EMPLOYEE NAME          MONTHLY SALARY   NEW SALARY
000017
000018      Department 500 Totals
000019      TOTAL                         1,500.00        1,575.00
000020      COUNT 1
000021
000022    600     BLACKBERG, KAREN        1,300.00        1,365.00
000023    600     SMITHE, CAROL           1,567.75        1,646.14
000024
000025      Department 600 Totals
000026      TOTAL                         2,867.75        3,011.14
000027      COUNT 2
000028
000029      End of Report Totals
000030      TOTAL                        12,136.50       12,743.33
000031      COUNT 8
****** ******* End of report ******
                                                                       Bottom
F3=Exit    F12=Cancel    F19=Left    F20=Right        F21=Split
```

Query has formatted the report subtotals for you. After each report break group is a blank line, followed by each selected summary function printed on a separate line. Notice that the actual department number has been included in the report break text, and that the End of Report Totals have not changed from file PAYMSTQ6.

Press	**F12**	to clear the report
Press	**F3**	to save the query as PAYMSTQ7, with an appropriate text description

When this report is printed, there will be one difference from previous reports. The printed version of a report break group prints the report break field. The department number will only print for the first person in the department. Therefore, Susan Powers will not have 100 to the left of her name, nor will John Klein and Gary Walker have 400 to the left of their names, and so on.

Review Questions

1. Explain the purpose of a report break.
2. How many report break levels are allowed by Query?
3. What one Query definition option *must* be selected before the report break option can be selected? Why?
4. How is a variable to be included in break text?

Exercises

1. Using file PAYMSTQ7, the query created in this chapter, print a report with the summaries and the break text suppressed at the department level. Save the report as CH7EX1.
2. Create a report break definition using the ADRMST file sequenced alphabetically by city name. Print a Query report that will list all cities, breaking on city name, and showing a count for each city. Include all fields in the detail information. Print the city name within the break text. Save the report as CH7EX2.
3. Create a report break definition using the ADRMST file sequenced by zip code. Design a Query report that will print only zip codes with a value greater than 30000, breaking on a change in zip code. Print all fields, except do not print the first two digits of the employee ID. Include the zip code within the break text. Save the report as CH7EX3.
4. Create a report break definition using the PAYMST file sequenced by department number. Design a Query report that will print all employees alphabetically within a department, printing department, name, and salary on a detail line. Sum the salary. Save the report as CH7EX4.

Chapter 8

Creating File Relationships

Objectives:

✓ To learn how to use more than one file in a Query definition

✓ To understand how to join files into a relation

Introduction

This chapter describes the use of more than one file in a Query definition. From the beginning of this text, all Query definitions have used only one file. Now that you understand what Query can do with data, you will be able to use more than one file as input.

In a relational database, data is organized in tables. These tables can then be linked by using a common field that exists in each table. On the AS/400, the term file is used instead of table. Multiple input files can be joined with one or more key fields to create a relation. Files can be joined to create relations within Query very simply. To accomplish the same joining process for other AS/400 high-level languages, a logical file with a Data Description Specification would first need to be created. In either case, you are creating an access path to the data. No actual file is ever created; therefore, no extra disk space is used and data does not become dated. After the files are joined, you may use any of the Query options to work with the data. For example, you may select only certain fields, select only certain records, define new fields, create a new file, and so on.

You are allowed to specify as many as 32 files to be joined. Each file is assigned a unique three-character identifier, Txx, where xx is a number from 1 to 32. The existing data names and the three-digit identifier are separated by a period. You can change the three-digit identifier if you would like one that is more meaningful. This identifier becomes a prefix to all field variable names, thus allowing the same field name to exist in more than one file. The identifier acts as a qualifier to make each field name unique to a particular file when you are specifying other options such as field selection, sorting, and result field definition.

The selected files are joined on identical key fields. For example, personnel and payroll files could be matched on an employee's social security number, which would exist in both files. Another example is a student file that contains course and section number, which could be matched on course and section number with the course file, which also contains the course name, section number, instructor, and classroom location for that section.

The chapter exercise will join the PAYMST and ADRMST files on employee ID to produce a report.

Joining Files

To begin a new query, access the Work with Queries menu, and select the Create function.

Press **Enter** to choose Specify file selections from the Define the Query menu

You are now at the Specify file selections screen, Figure 8.1, where you specify one or more database files that you want your query to read. Because the data files you have been using are in your library, you have not needed to also specify library, member name, and record format. However, these items are often necessary and should not be ignored.

Figure 8.1
Specify File Selections Screen

```
                              Specify File Selections

Type choices, press Enter.  Press F9 to specify an additional
  file selection.

File . . . . . . . __________       Name, F4 for list
  Library  . . . .   yourname       Name, *LIBL, F4 for list
Member . . . . . . *FIRST           Name, *FIRST, F4 for list
Format . . . . . . *FIRST           Name, *FIRST, F4 for list













                                                                  Bottom
F3=Exit          F4=Prompt          F5=Report          F9=Add file
F12=Cancel       F13=Layout         F24=More keys
```

Use the physical file name PAYMST as the first input file name.

Type **PAYMST** as the file name
Press **Enter** to accept the library, member, and format defaults

Query will display the following message to verify the file name: `Select file(s), or press Enter to confirm.` You must now select the additional file.

Press **F9** to specify an additional file selection

You now have another file selection section on your screen.

Type	**ADRMST**	as the second file name
Press	**Enter**	to accept the library, member, and format defaults

Your screen should now match Figure 8.2.

Figure 8.2
Specify File Selections — Options Completed

```
                         Specify File Selections

Type choices, press Enter.  Press F9 to specify an additional
  file selection.

File . . . . . . . . PAYMST          Name, F4 for list
  Library  . . . .     yourname      Name, *LIBL, F4 for list
Member . . . . . . . *FIRST          Name, *FIRST, F4 for list
Format . . . . . . . PAYMSTR         Name, *FIRST, F4 for list
File ID  . . . . . . T01             A-Z99, *ID

File . . . . . . . . ADRMST          Name, F4 for list
  Library  . . . .     yourname      Name, *LIBL, F4 for list
Member . . . . . . . *FIRST          Name, *FIRST, F4 for list
Format . . . . . . . ADRMSTR         Name, *FIRST, F4 for list
File ID  . . . . . . T02             A-Z99, *ID



                                                            Bottom
F3=Exit        F4=Prompt      F5=Report        F9=Add file
F12=Cancel     F13=Layout     F24=More keys
Select file(s), or press Enter to confirm
```

Note that PAYMST has been assigned a File ID of T01 and ADRMST has been assigned a File ID of T02. You may press F9 up to 30 more times to join the maximum number of files (32).

Press	**Enter**	to confirm the selection of these files

You must now indicate the method for joining the files, and the fields that will be used to join the two files. On the Specify Type of Join screen are three options for joining (see Figure 8.3).

Option 1, Matched records, only selects records where there is an exact key match on the files that have been selected. For a record to be selected, all the files must have a matching field as defined in the join specification (the next screen). An example of this option would be the match of personnel and payroll records using the employee ID field. The personnel file contains the employee address field. The payroll file contains only employee payroll data. Checks must be mailed to employees. Therefore, the address must be obtained by matching the two files on employee ID to extract the address from the employee's personnel record. The only records selected will be for those employees with matching employee ID on both files. There is no primary file with Option 1, because matching fields must exist on all files selected to create a joined record.

Figure 8.3
Specify Type of Join Screen

```
                          Specify Type of Join

Type choice, press Enter.

  Type of join . . . . 1          1=Matched records
                                  2=Matched records with primary file
                                  3=Unmatched records with primary









F3=Exit         F5=Report        F10=Process/previous
F12=Cancel      F13=Layout       F18=Files
```

Every file that is selected in Option 1 is treated equally, but the output sequence may vary. Therefore, you should use the Query sort option to assure a correctly sequenced output.

Options 2 and 3 use a primary file that is matched to one or more secondary files. The first file selected on the Specify File Selections screen is considered the primary file as the default. If you want another sequence, you must select the sort options. All other files are considered secondary. The output will be sequenced by the primary file. When you select more than one secondary file, the primary file is matched with the first secondary file. The combined output is then matched with the next secondary file, and so on. Therefore, the order in which files are selected is very important when you are using options 2 and 3.

Option 2, Matched records with primary file, selects all primary file records and includes any secondary file records that match the field(s) specified in the join specifications. This might be the better option to use for the address match of payroll and personnel files. If for some reason a new employee had not been entered on the personnel file, he or she would not receive a paycheck when using option 1, because only records that appear on both files are selected. This second option selects all primary file records, and includes the secondary file record if it exists. Therefore, the new employee's paycheck would print with a blank address.

Option 3, Unmatched records with primary file, selects only primary file records that have no match with secondary file records on the specified key field. You could run this option before paycheck processing to determine whether or not there are records on the payroll file that do not match records on the personnel file. These non-matches could then be displayed or printed and the employees' address information added to the personnel file before the paycheck address query is executed.

For this chapter's exercise, the join will be on matched records.

Press	**Enter**	to accept the default of option 1

The next screen, Figure 8.4, is used to designate the field(s) that will be used to join the files. You can specify up to 100 join tests, but each must evaluate as true for Query to select the records. The relational operators are: equal, not equal, less than, greater than, less than or equal, and greater than or equal. You will select the fields from the list at the bottom of the screen.

TIP: To see more fields, move the cursor to the bottom half of the screen and use Shift/Roll Up.

TIP: Remember that the three-character extension and the separating period must be used with the field name. For example, T01.EMPID.

Figure 8.4
Specify How To Join Files Screen

```
                          Specify How to Join Files

Type comparisons to show how file selections are related, press Enter. Tests: EQ, NE,
  LE, GE, LT, GT

Field                Test         Field
________________     _____        ______________
________________     _____        ______________
________________     _____        ______________
________________     _____        ______________
________________     _____        ______________
                                                                            Bottom
.....................................................................................
Field          Text                                        Len  Dec
T01.EMPID      EMP ID                                        4
T01.DEPTNO     DEPT NO                                       3
T01.NAME       EMPLOYEE NAME                                20
T01.MONSAL     MONTHLY SALARY                                6    2
T02.EMPID      EMP ID                                        4
                                                                          More...
F3=Exit        F5=Report        F10=Proc/prev       F11=Display
F12=Cancel     F13=Layout       F18=Files           F24=More keys
```

For the chapter exercise, match the files on employee ID and print a report in employee ID sequence. Enter the following:

Type	**T01.EMPID**	in the first field
Press	**Field Exit**	
Type	**EQ**	for the test
Press	**Field Exit**	
Type	**T02.EMPID**	in the second field
Press	**Enter**	

You will return to the Define the Query menu.

Type	1	to choose the Select sort fields option. Type a 1 in sort priority for the employee ID field.

Press	**Enter**	to return to the menu
Press	**F5**	to run the Query

Your report should match Figures 8.5 and 8.6.

Figure 8.5
Display Report Screen, Columns 1-55

```
                                    Display Report
                                                           Report width . . .127
Position to line . . .              Shift to column  . . . . . . .__
Line      ....+....1....+....2....+....3....+....4....+....5....+..
          EMP ID  DEPT NO  EMPLOYEE NAME    MONTHLY SALARY  EMP ID
000001    1234      400    JONES, BILL          1,322.00      1234
000002    1892      500    TUCKER, MARY         1,500.00      1892
000003    2567      100    ADAMS, MARK          1,546.50      2567
000004    3567      600    SMITHE, CAROL        1,567.75      3567
000005    4672      600    BLACKBERG, KAREN     1,300.00      4672
000006    5632      200    GREEN, TOM           1,200.00      5632
000007    5718      300    HART, BOB            1,222.00      5718
000008    6340      100    POWERS, SUSAN        1,725.00      6340
000009    7290      400    KLEIN, JOHN          1,400.00      7290
******    ******   End of report   ******

                                                                         Bottom
F3-Exit      F12-Cancel      F19-Left      F20-Right          F21-Split
```

Figure 8.6
Display Report Screen, Columns 56-112

```
                                    Display Report
                                                           Report width . . .127
Position to line . . .             Shift to column  . . . . . . .__
Line      ....6....+....7....+....8....+....9....+...10....+...11..
          EMP ID  STREET              CITY      STATE  ZIP CD  PHON
000001    1234    639 JEFFERSON #110  BOSTON     MA    01021   6175
000002    1892    8562 VAN BUREN      PORTLAND   OR    97827   5038
000003    2567    8462 CARTER BLVD    PORTLAND   OR    97811   5038
000004    3567    784 MONROE          PORTLAND   OR    97822   5038
000005    4672    8462 JACKSON        BOSTON     MA    01022   6175
000006    5632    4549 MADISON AVE    BOSTON     MA    01022   6175
000007    5718    7353 ADAMS          PORTLAND   OR    98701   5038
000008    6340    2698 POLK           PORTLAND   OR    97812   5038
000009    7290    610 WASHINGTON #6   BOSTON     MA    01002   6175
******    ******   End of report   ******

                                                                         Bottom
F3-Exit      F12-Cancel      F19-Left      F20-Right          F21-Split
Last column of report.
```

TIP: Note that this particular report is 127 columns wide. The width of one display screen is 80 columns. To view data that is to the right, press F20. Press F19 to return to the data that is displayed on the left.

A review of the output will verify any errors made in the employee ID. You should have only nine employees listed. These records demonstrate that the join is only on matched employee IDs. Gary Walker's employee ID is 0516 on the PAYMST file and there is no match on the ADRMST file. The

3516 employee ID could be a data entry error, and it may be Gary Walker's address. Also note that all fields from both files print.

TIP: When files are joined, you should select the fields for printing, because you would not want both key fields to print. See Figure 8.5 and note that the first and last columns are EMP ID.

Press	**F12**	to exit this screen
Press	**F3**	to access the save and exit screen

Save this Query as file PAYMSTQ8 with appropriate text.

Review Questions

1. What are the benefits of using joined files?
2. Explain the three options for joining files in Query.
3. If up to 100 join tests are specified, and each must be true for a record to be selected, is this AND or OR logic?
4. Access a Display Report screen by running a query. Place the cursor on the function key line and press the HELP key. What does the F21 key do?

Exercises

1. Using the query created in this chapter, PAYMSTQ8, print only name, street, city, state, and phone number, in name sequence. Save the report as CH8EX1.
2. Join files PAYMST and DPTMST as matched records on department number. List each employee name and salary within department name. This is not a control break report. Save the report as CH8EX2.
3. Join the PAYMST, ADRMST, and DPTMST files as matched records. Join the PAYMST and ADRMST files on employee ID, and the PAYMST and DPTMST files on department number. Print a control break report listing department name, employee name, employee ID, monthly salary, and phone number.

   Sum monthly salary by department. Print the final total of monthly salary.

   The report must be in sequence by employee name within department name, printing each department name on the break. Format the phone number as XXX-XXX-XXXX. Save the report as CH8EX3.
4. Join PAYMST and ADRMST on employee ID, using a join of unmatched records with the primary file. Save the report as CH8EX4.
5. Join files PAYMST and ADRMST on employee ID, using a join of matched records with the primary file. Save the report as CH8EX5.

Chapter 9

Report Column Formatting

Objectives:

- ✓ To learn how to control the format of Query output
- ✓ To learn how to edit numeric fields

Introduction

This chapter describes how to change the spacing between report columns, how to specify new column headings, how to change output field lengths, and how to control the editing of numeric output fields. The Specify report column formatting option allows you to specify these items.

Column Formatting

The first exercise in this chapter will be to use the column options. You may change the number of spaces to the left of each column. The Query default for column spacing is no spaces in front of the first column, and two spaces between remaining columns. The default column width is determined by the length of the field or the length of the default column heading, whichever is larger.

You may also change the column heading text from the default. Default column headings have been provided for you by an externally defined record description, created with Data Description Specifications (DDS). Column headings may also be defined by Interactive Data Definition Utility (IDDU) field definitions. (See the *Query/400 User's Guide* (SC41-9614), *DFU User's Guide and Reference* (SC09-1381), and *Learning about Office Vision/400 Word Processing* (SC41-9617) for additional information.) If there were no default column headings, Query would use the field name. This option allows you to change these headings, providing up to three lines of heading for a column. Remember that you created column headings for the fields you created when you were defining result fields (in Chapter 3). These column headings may also be changed.

You can also change the size of output fields. You can lengthen or shorten both character and numeric fields. The length of the decimal position also can be changed in numeric fields. To omit a field in the output, change the field length to zero. You may need to use this method of not printing a field when the field must be used by other Query options, such as sort, record selection, report break, or join.

For example, when you are creating a Query with report breaks, the file must be in the break field sequence, and therefore that field must be selected. This selected field will print on each detail line. See Figure 7.6 for an example of control breaks by department. The department number is repeated on each line and also prints in the break text. To suppress the department number printing on each detail line, set the DEPTNO field length to zero on the Specify report column formatting screen. None of these changes affects the fields in the file. These changes are only for report or database Query output.

You will use the Query definition PAYMSTQ8 as the basis of the new report. Access the Work with Queries menu, and select the Change function for PAYMSTQ8.

Press	**F5**	to display the report to review its contents

See Figures 8.5 and 8.6 to be certain you have the correct query from Chapter 8. If your report does not match, reference Chapter 8 to determine your error.

Press	**F12**	to return to the menu

This report contains 10 columns of data. The employee ID is displayed in two columns because both files contain this field. The following chapter exercise will consist of improving the format of this report.

Before the column formatting is changed, T02.EMPID needs to be omitted from the detail line. The output fields must be resequenced so that they print left to right: employee name, employee ID, department, salary, street, city, state, zip, and phone. The phone number must be printed in the format XXX-XXX-XXXX.

Type	1	to choose the Define result fields option to reformat the phone number using the substring and concatenation operators. Use NEWPHONE as the new phone number field name.
Press	**Enter**	to return to the menu
Type	1	to choose the Select and sequence fields option to omit T02.EMPID, T02.PHONE, and any substring working fields. Resequence the remaining fields.
Press	**Enter**	to return to the menu
Press	**F5**	to run the report and display the results on your screen

Note the new report format and that you have used 121 positions. You may print 132 characters. Therefore, in the chapter exercises you will adjust some of the spacing between the columns of data. You will also change the column headings and the numeric editing of the monthly salary.

Press	**F12**	to return to the menu
Type	**1**	to choose Specify report column formatting
Press	**Enter**	to see the Specify Report Column Formatting Screen (Figure 9.1)

Figure 9.1
Specify Report Column Formatting Screen

```
                         Specify Report Column Formatting

Type information, press Enter.
 Column headings: *NONE, aligned text lines

                Column
Field           Spacing     Column Heading             Len     Dec     Edit
T01.NAME           0        EMPLOYEE NAME_______        20
                            ____________________
                            ____________________

T01.EMPID          2        EMP ID______________         4
                            ____________________
                            ____________________

T02.DEPTNO         2        DEPT NO_____________         3
                            ____________________
                            ____________________

                                                                   More...
F3=Exit         F5=Report      F10=Process/prev      F12=Cancel
F13=Layout      F16=Edit       F18=Files             F23=Long comment
```

The Query default for column spacing is two spaces between each field based on whichever is longer, field length or heading length. To change this default, type a new value on top of the existing value.

To change the existing column headings, you have two options. You may specify no headings for a field by typing *NONE (this must be uppercase) in the Column Heading area. The second option is to type up to three lines of text, with a maximum of 20 characters each, in the Column Heading area.

TIP: If you change your mind and want to return to the original default heading, blank out the text in the Column Heading area with the Field Exit key or the space bar.

You have three screens of field information to format for the nine reporting fields. For the chapter exercise, you will change every heading, using uppercase and lowercase. Use the instructions in Figure 9.2 for each field. Note that the second line of heading text has leading spaces to force the heading text to be centered. Change the column spacing only for the designated fields.

Figure 9.2
Instructions To Reformat Column Spacing and Change Headings

Field Name	New Spacing	New Heading
NAME	4	Employee Name
EMPID		Employee ID
DEPTNO		Department Number
MONSAL	3	Monthly Salary
STREET		Street
CITY		City
STATE		State
ZIP	3	Zip Code
NEWPHONE	3	Phone

Editing Numeric Fields

Query has been editing numeric fields based on the Query defaults. You may change the default editing by defining your own editing. The Edit column on the Specify Report Column Formatting screen will show an asterisk if there are editing overrides.

TIP: You cannot edit character fields with the Specify Report Column Formatting option. Character fields can only be edited with the Define result fields Query option.

To edit a numeric field, position the cursor on the field and press F16 to go to the Define Numeric Field Editing screen. For the chapter exercise, do the following:

Position	**the cursor**	on the monthly salary field
Press	**F16**	for Edit

You will now see the Define Numeric Field Editing screen, Figure 9.3. This is the first of two screens to indicate the type of editing you want to use. The top half of the screen shows the current editing information for the field, including the original heading text and your revised heading lines. This screen also shows an example of the current editing for monthly salary. You now have four options for editing.

Option 1 provides more numeric editing options, including the position of the negative sign and whether or not to print a dollar sign. Option 2 allows you to select the separator character for date and time fields. Options 3 and 4 provide an edit code and edit words for numeric editing similar to codes available in RPG/400. We will cover only options 1 and 2 in this text. Refer to the *Query/400 User's Guide* for more information about options 3 and 4.

Press	**Enter**	to transfer to the Describe Numeric Field Editing screen (Figure 9.4).

Figure 9.3
Define Numeric Field Editing Screen

```
                          Define Numeric Field Editing

Field . . . . . . . :    T01.MONSAL
Text  . . . . . . . :    MONTHLY SALARY
Heading 1 . . . . . :    Monthly
Heading 2 . . . . . :    Salary
Heading 3 . . . . . :
Length  . . . . . . :    6
Decimal . . . . . . :    2
Sample  . . . . . . :    9,999.99


Type choice, press Enter.

 Edit option . . . . 1             1-Numeric editing choices
                                   2-Date or time editing choice
                                   3-Edit code
                                   4-Edit word

F3-Exit        F5-Report      F10-Process/prev       F11-Chg sample
F12-Cancel     F13-Layout     F16-Remove Edit        F18-Files
```

Figure 9.4
Describe Numeric Field Editing Screen

```
                         Describe Numeric Field Editing

Field   . . . . . . . :  T01.MONSAL


Type choices, press Enter.

 Decimal point . . . . . . . 1          1-.  2-,  3-:  4-$     5-None
 Thousands separator . . . . 2          1-.  2-,  3-'  4-Blank 5-None
 Show negative sign  . . . . Y          Y-Yes, N-No
   Left negative sign. . . . _____
   Right negative sign . . . _____
 Show currency symbol  . . . N          Y-Yes, N-No
   Left currency symbol. . . $____
   Right currency symbol . . _____
 Print zero value  . . . . . Y          Y-Yes, N-No
 Replace leading zeros . . . Y          Y-Yes, N-No
   Replace with  . . . . . . 1             1-Blanks
                                        2-Asterisks
                                        3-Floating currency symbol
   Single leading zero . . . N          Y-Yes, N-No

F3-Exit         F5-Report           F10-Process/prev        F12-Cancel
F13-Layout      F16-Remove Edit     F18-Files
```

The values shown for each of the choices are the Query defaults. For example, MONSAL will print with a decimal point that looks like a period; the thousands separator will be a comma; a negative sign will print to the right of the value if the value is negative; no currency symbol will print; if the value is zero, a zero will print; and leading zeros will be replaced with blanks. You may now change any of these choices.

The decimal point is typical for U.S. currency, but you may change it. You could eliminate the thousands separator if you needed to save space because you have a wide report. If you prefer no negative sign, or the sign on the left of the value, you may change the Show negative sign choices. From 1 to 6 characters can be printed to the left or right of a negative value. For example, you can enter CR AMT at the negative sign choice, and a negative value would have those characters printed to the left or right, depending on your selection.

To print a dollar sign, change the Show currency symbol option from N to Y. The $ will then print to the left of the value, at the left edge of the field width. Therefore, if MONSAL value is 100, the output would print as $__100.00, where the __ indicates two spaces. The dollar sign will print next to the high-order digit if you change the Replace leading zeros option to a 3.

TIP: The $ takes another space in the field, so the field requires an additional position to print.

If you prefer blanks to print when a value is zero, change the Print zero value option to N. The Replace leading zeros option may be set to "no" to have the leading zeros print with the value. MONSAL would then print as 00100.00. You can also replace the leading zeros with asterisks, or with the floating dollar sign. MONSAL would print as **100.00 with the leading zeros replaced with asterisks. MONSAL would print as __$100.00 with the leading zeros replaced with the floating currency symbol.

TIP: If you do not like the editing choices, use F16 to remove the currently defined edit selections and begin again.

See the *Query/400 User's Guide* for other combinations of these numeric field editing choices.

For this chapter exercise, you will add a currency symbol to the report and choose a floating dollar sign for the salary.

Press	**Tab**	repeatedly to bypass the choices down to Show currency symbol
Type	**Y**	for Show currency symbol
Press	**Tab**	to bypass the choices down to Replace leading zeros
Type	**3**	for the Replace with option
Press	**Enter**	to return to the previous screen
Press	**Enter**	to return to the Define the Query menu and save the editing choices
Press	**F5**	to run the report interactively to the screen.

You should save this new Query definition as PAYMSTQ9; run it in batch and print the output.

Editing Date and Time Fields

As neither the PAYMST, ADRMST, nor DPTMST file contains a numeric date field, there is no field available for you to practice this editing. Figure 9.5 is the date and time editing screen.

Fields that contain date or time must be defined as numeric to allow this editing. You may choose the separator for the 6-digit date field so that the date prints as mm/dd/yy or mm-dd-yy. A time field that includes hours, minutes, and seconds could be edited to print as hh:mm:ss or hh.mm.ss.

Figure 9.5
Describe Date and Time Editing Screen

```
                         Describe Date/Time Field Editing
Field . . . . . . :

Type choice, press Enter.

  Date/Time separator . . . _        1=.  2=/  3=:  4=-  5=,





F3=Exit          F5=Report               F10=Process/prev      F12=Cancel
F13=Layout       F16=Remove Edit         F18=Files
```

If your date or time field is defined as a character field, you will need to use the substring and concatenation commands on the Define Result Fields screen to edit the field. If your date or time field is defined as a date or time data type, the output format is predefined. See Appendix C and the *Query/400 User's Guide* for more information on data types.

Review Questions

1. What advantages does the report column formatting option have over the Query defaults?
2. What are the column spacing defaults?
3. Describe the steps to edit a numeric field.
4. Describe the steps to edit a numeric date or time field.
5. How do you remove numeric edits after defining them with the Define Numeric Editing option?

Review Questions

1. Use file CH8EX1 from Chapter 8. Change this Query definition to have 10 spaces between columns, and no column headings. Save the report as CH9EX1.
2. Use file CH8EX2 from Chapter 8. Change this Query definition to print two lines of column headings, using uppercase and lowercase (similar to the Chapter 9 exercise). Save the report as CH9EX2.
3. Use file CH8EX3 from Chapter 8. Change this Query definition to calculate three new raise fields of 3 percent, 5 percent, and 7 percent with a length of six spaces and two decimals. The amount of the raise must not be added to the salary. The raise fields should reflect only the amount of the raise. Headings should be "3 Percent Raise" and so on.

   Edit the 3 percent field to print with leading zeroes as asterisks. Edit the 5 percent field to print with a floating dollar sign. Edit the 7 percent field to print with a fixed dollar sign. Total each of these fields. Print these new fields to the right of monthly salary.

   Print the monthly salary with no thousands separator. Do not print the department name on the detail line.

   Save this Query as CH9EX3.

Chapter 10

Selecting Output Type and Form

Objectives:

- ✓ To learn how to format reports for the printer
- ✓ To learn how to output database files

Introduction

This chapter describes how to enhance printed output and how to create a database as output. You have been displaying Query definitions on the screen and printing the same format. You have been using the Query defaults for line spacing and form size, and the reports have had no page headings. The Select output type and output form option allows you to modify these items.

Printed Output Formatting

The first exercise in this chapter will be to use the printer options. You will be using the original PAYMST physical file for the report. To begin a new Query, access the Work with Queries menu, and select the Create function. Select PAYMST on the Specify file selections screen.

Type	**1**	to choose Select output type and output form
Press	**Enter**	

Figure 10.1 is an example of the screen you will see.

Figure 10.1
Select Output Type and Output Form Screen

```
                    Select Output Type and Output Form

Type choices, press Enter.

  Output type . . . . . . .    1      1=Display
                                      2=Printer
                                      3=Database file

  Form of output  . . . . .    1      1=Detail
                                      2=Summary only

  Line wrapping . . . . . .    N      Y=Yes, N=No
     Wrapping width . . . .   ___     Blank, 1-378
     Record on one page . .    N      Y=Yes, N=No




F3=Exit          F5=Report          F10=Process/previous
F12=Cancel       F13=Layout         F18=Files
```

The three choices available on this screen determine which additional screens you will view. The defaults are presented to you: a display output with detail lines and no line wrapping. If you make no changes, you will return to the menu when you press Enter and exit this screen.

The choice of Output type has three options. The first option is to display the output on the screen (display). This option may seem rather obvious, because you have easily displayed your output using F5 on the Define the Query screen. However, you could use this option in conjunction with the Form of output option to display a normal detail report with only summaries. If a Query definition with the report break option was lengthy, and you needed to check the summary level totals before printing, then you could use this option to display the report breaks on the screen. You could press F5 to immediately display the summaries on the screen.

The second Output type option is to send the output to a spooled file. You have already been using this concept by having Query run in batch. This selection causes other screens to be presented that allow you to further define how the output will be printed.

We will cover the third Output type option, to create a database file, later in this chapter.

The choice of Form of output has two options. The default detail option prints, or writes to a file, all the records. The summary option prints, or writes to a file, only the report breaks and final totals. If you had created a report break definition that printed the detail, this option would easily allow you to print another version of the same report with only summary information.

The third choice, Line wrapping, contains three options that are for printed output only. When the total width of the fields to be printed is wider than the specified width of the paper, you may specify that these long lines wrap to the next line, or be truncated. If you specify lines to be wrapped, you may choose the maximum width of the lines to be printed in the report. This

Wrapping width is better left blank, so that Query wraps the best it can. When line wrapping is requested, if a record begins to print at a page break, you may then prevent wrapped records from being split on two pages by specifying that a record print on one page. For the chapter exercise, use the following options:

Type	**2**	to send the report to the printer
Press	**Enter**	to bypass the remaining options

When the output type is modified for the printer, information about the printer must then be provided. See Figure 10.2, the Define Printer Output screen.

Figure 10.2
Define Printer Output Screen

```
                          Define Printer Output

Type choices, press Enter.

  Printer device  . . . . .      *PRINT      *PRINT, name

  Form size
    Length  . . . . . . . .      ___            Blank, 1-255
    Width . . . . . . . . .      132            Blank, 1-378

  Start line  . . . . . . .      ___            Blank, 1-255

  End line  . . . . . . . .      ___            Blank, 1-255

  Line spacing  . . . . . .      1              1, 2, 3

  Print definition  . . . .      N              Y=Yes, N=No



F3=Exit          F5=Report          F10=Process/previous
F12=Cancel       F13=Layout         F18=Files
```

This screen is used to define the printer device and the characteristics of the paper used in the printer. In a classroom situation, you will use the printer defaults for the printer device, form size, start line, and end line. You can change spacing to double (2) or triple (3) space. You can also request that the Query definition be printed with the report. A Query definition is a minimum two-page listing of all of the Query options used by this query. The definition prints defined result fields, sort fields, headings, and so on.

For this report, the defaults are acceptable.

Press	**Enter**	to accept the Define Printer Output defaults

The next options are on the Define Spooled Output screen. See Figure 10.3 for an example of this screen.

Figure 10.3
Define Spooled Output Screen

```
                         Define Spooled Output

Type choices, press Enter.

  Spool the output . . . .  _          Blank, Y-Yes, N-No

  Form type . . . . . . . . ___        Blank, name, *STD

  Copies. . . . . . . . .   1          Blank, 1-255

  Hold  . . . . . . . . .   _          Blank, Y-Yes, N-No



F3-Exit          F5-Report          F10-Process/previous
F12-Cancel       F13-Layout         F18-Files
```

Because the output default is to create a spooled file, you will leave the options on this screen at their defaults. Form type refers to an actual form name that would exist in a specific working environment. Copies is the number of times this report should print. Hold refers to a working environment where output is often held and must then be manually released for printing by the operator.

Press **Enter** to accept all the defaults

Your next option is to define a cover page on the Specify Cover Page screen (Figure 10.4). A cover page is a separate page at the beginning of a Query report that contains the name of the query, its library, the file(s) used,

Figure 10.4
Specify Cover Page Screen

```
                          Specify Cover Page

Type choices, press Enter.

  Print cover page . . . .    Y          Y-Yes, N-No

  Cover page title
________________________________________________________________________
________________________________________________________________________
________________________________________________________________________



F3-Exit          F5-Report          F10-Process/previous
F12-Cancel       F13-Layout         F18-Files
```

and the date and time it was run. This cover page has been an automatic feature of running Query in batch mode. Now you can add up to four lines of text to title the report. You also can suppress printing of this page. Although the cover page is an optional page, this page helps users and students locate the proper listings, and it is very helpful in a classroom situation.

The title text will be printed above the standard cover page text. Both uppercase and lowercase settings are acceptable. You can enter up to a maximum of four lines for title text.

For this chapter exercise, enter the following.

Press	**Tab**	to accept the "yes" for the cover page
Type	**your name**	on the first cover page title line
Press	**Enter**	

The last printing option available is to define page headings and footings on the Specify Page Headings and Footings screen (Figure 10.5). Query provides a standard page heading that contains the system date and time, and the page number. This is always the first line of every page. The date and time print on the top left of every page. The word PAGE and current page number print on the top right of every page. This heading information stays within the width of your printed line. Therefore, if a detail line is 40 characters wide, the date, time, and page number are within 40 characters. If a line is 120 characters wide, the date, time, and page number are within the 120 characters.

Figure 10.5
Specify Page Headings and Footings Screen

```
                    Specify Page Headings and Footings

Type choices, press Enter.
  (Type &date, &time, and &page, or choose standard headings.)

  Print standard
    page headings . . . .    Y          Y-Yes, N-No

  Page heading
______________________________________________________________________
______________________________________________________________________
______________________________________________________________________

  Page footing
______________________________________________________________________




F3-Exit          F5-Report          F10-Process/previous
F12-Cancel       F13-Layout         F18-Files
```

You can specify your own heading text and keep the standard page headings for date, time, and page. Your text will be centered between the standard information. The heading will be truncated if it will not fit. The other two heading lines, if present, are printed below the first line.

You also can design your own page heading text and control the placement of the date, time, and page number. The Query variable names `&date`, `&time`, and `&page` contain the date, time, and page number values. By using these variables in your heading text, you control the placement of these fields. If you want the word PAGE (or Page) to precede the page number value, you must type the word PAGE (or Page) before the variable `&page`.

A footing prints on the last line of text on every page. The footing may contain text and the date, time, and page number.

TIP: You can use the variables for date, time, and page number only once on a page. They will not print in both a header and a footer.

For this chapter exercise, enter the following:

Type	**N**	to not print the standard heading for date, time, and page number
Type	**PAYMST report for &date &time**	as the Page heading text on line one
Press	**Field Exit**	
Type	**Page &page**	at the right end of line two
Press	**Field Exit**	
Press	**Field Exit**	to exit the third heading line
Type	**This is a footing**	as the Page footing text
Press	**Enter**	

You cannot see the headings and footings that you created with this Select output type and output form option if you press F5 to run an interactive query. Save this query as PAYMSTQ10 to run in batch mode. Display the spool file to be certain that you have the required headings and footings. Print the correct report output.

Selecting Output for a Database File

You will create a new database file from the PAYMST file for the second exercise in this chapter. The new file will have only two fields, employee ID and monthly salary. To begin a new query, access the Work with Queries menu, and select the Create function. Select PAYMST on the Specify File Selections screen.

Type	**1**	to choose Select and sequence fields. Select empid and monsal fields.
Press	**Enter**	
Type	**1**	to choose Select output type and output form
Press	**Enter**	

See Figure 10.6 for the Select Output screen.

Figure 10.6
Select Output Type and Output Form Screen

```
                 Select Output Type and Output Form

Type choices, press Enter.

  Output type . . . . . . .    1      1=Display
                                      2=Printer
                                      3=Database file

  Form of output  . . . . .    1      1=Detail
                                      2=Summary only

  Line wrapping . . . . . .    N      Y=Yes, N=No
     Wrapping width . . . .   ____    Blank, 1-378
     Record on one page . .    N      Y=Yes, N=No






F3=Exit           F5=Report          F10=Process/previous
F12=Cancel        F13=Layout         F18=Files
```

For the chapter exercise, enter the following:

Type	**3**	to select Database file
Press	**Enter**	to accept the remaining defaults

When a database file is selected as the output type on the Select Output Type and Output Form screen, your file options are chosen from the Define Database File Output screen. See Figure 10.7 for an example of this screen.

Figure 10.7
Define Database File Output Screen

```
                        Define Database File Output

Type choices, press Enter.
  (The printed definition shows the output file record layout.)

  File . . . . . . . . . .  QQRYOUT                Name, F4 for list
    Library  . . . . . . .     yourname            Name, F4 for list
  Member . . . . . . . . .  *FILE                  Name, *FIRST, *F....

  Data in file . . . . . .  1                      1=New file,2=Replace
                                                   file,3=New member,
                                                   4=Replace member,
                                                   5=Add to member

  For a new file:
    Authority  . . . . . .  *LIBCRTAUT             *LIBCRTAUT, *CHANGE
                                                   *ALL, *EXCLUDE, *USE
                                                   authorization list..
    Text . . . . . . . . .  _____________________________________________
  Print definition . . . .  N                      Y=Yes, N=No

F3=Exit           F4=Prompt          F5=Report          F10=Process/previous
F12=Cancel        F13=Layout         F18=Files
```

On this screen you specify the name of the output file and its library. You also must specify whether or not this is a new file, a new member for an existing file, and whether or not this data is adding to an existing member or replacing an existing file or member. No file checks are made by the system until the query is run. You must be certain that the Data in file option is correct.

For example, if you select option 2, to replace a file, and the file does not exist, your query run will abort. Also, if you need to rerun a file output query, you *must* change the Data in file option to 2 because the file already exists. Query cannot create a file again. The file must be replaced.

The authority value specifies the kind of object authority you want to give other users of your database file. The default of *LIBCRTAUT assigns the same authority value from the library the object is being created into. *CHANGE, *ALL, *EXCLUDE, and *USE are the usual AS/400 authorities.

TIP: File names are composed of nine alphanumeric characters (A through Z, 0 through 9). Do not begin file names with a Q, because AS/400 system-supplied file names start with a Q. For this chapter exercise, create a file name of PFILEQ1 for the new file.

Type	**PFILEQ1**	for the File name
Press	**Field Exit**	
Press	**Tab**	to bypass your library name, member, option 1 for Data in a file, and authority
Type	**First PAYMST Query file**	for the text
Press	**Field Exit**	
Type	**Y**	to print the new file definition
Press	**Enter**	to return to the Define the Query menu
Press	**F3**	to begin the save process

Save this Query definition as PAYMSTQF1, to denote that this is the first file definition for the PAYMST file. Print the QPQUPRFIL output, which is only the file definition. To actually view the data in the file, you must display the file's contents.

Type	**WRKOBJPDM**	on any command line
Find	**PFILEQ1**	your new *FILE object, with an attribute of PF-DTA
Type	**12**	on the option line
Press	**Enter**	to access the Member screen
Type	**5**	on the option line
Press	**Enter**	to display the member

TIP: A shortcut to view the file is to type DSPPFM (the Display Physical File Member command) on any command line and prompt with F4. Type the file name (PFILEQ1) and press Enter. Also see Appendix A for more information.

You should now see the data shown in Figure 10.8. Note that data file output contains no editing. The EMPID field is in positions 1-4, and the MONSAL field is in positions 5-10.

Figure 10.8
Display Physical File Member Screen

```
                              Display Physical File Member
File . . . . . . :   PFILEQ1            Library  . . . :   yourname
Member . . . . . :   PFILEQ1            Record . . . . :   1
Control  . . . .     ________           Column . . . . :   1
Find . . . . . .     ___________________________________
*...+....1
1234132200
3567156775
5632120000
2567154650
4672130000
7290140000
1892150000
6516177525
6340172500
5718122200
                        ****** END OF DATA ******


                                                                         Bottom
F3-Exit      F12-Cancel     F19-Left      F20-Right       F24-More keys
```

Use the CPYF command to print a copy of this data.

Type	**CPYF**	on any command line
Press	**F4**	
Type	**PFILEQ1**	as the From file name
Press	**Tab**	to bypass the library
Type	***PRINT**	as the To file name
Press	**Enter**	

You now have a file named QSYSPRT in your output queue. This is a listing of the PFILEQ1 data file.

Review Questions

1. Explain why the Select Output Type and Form definition should be used for printed Query reports.
2. Explain the difference between a standard page heading and a user-defined page heading.
3. Define a cover page. Why is it useful?
4. Explain the difference between a detail report and a summary report.
5. Why would you need/want to create another file?

Exercises

1. Using file PAYMSTQ7 from Chapter 7, print only the summary information and also print a definition of the query. Include a suitable cover page, column headings, and page headings. Use the standard page heading with your heading text. Save the report as CH10EX1.
2. Output the summary fields from Exercise 1 to a file. Save the file as CH10EX2F. Save the query as CH10EX2. Print the file data using the CPYF command.
3. Using file PAYMSTQ6 from Chapter 6, print the report with a page heading that includes your name. A footer must contain the date, time, and page number. Save the report as CH10EX3.
4. Using file PAYMSTQ3 from Chapter 3, create a database file that has employee ID, monthly salary, new salary, and address fields from ADRMST (street, city, state, and zip). Save the file as CH10EX4F. Save the query as CH10EX4. Print the file data using the CPYF command. PAYMST must be the primary file.

Appendix A

Data Files and the Display Physical File Command

PAYMST File

The example Payroll Master File fields used in this text are the following:

Field Name	Field Description	Data Type
EMPID	Employee ID number	four alphanumeric characters
DEPTNO	Department number	three alphanumeric characters
NAME	Employee name	20 alphanumeric characters
MONSAL	Monthly salary amount	six numeric characters with two decimal positions (9999.99)

The data in the PAYMST file are the following:

EMPID	DEPTNO	NAME	MONSAL
1234	400	JONES, BILL	1322.00
3567	600	SMITHE, CAROL	1567.75
5632	200	GREEN, TOM	1200.00
2567	100	ADAMS, MARK	1546.50
4672	600	BLACKBERG, KAREN	1300.00
7290	400	KLEIN, JOHN	1400.00
1892	500	TUCKER, MARY	1500.00
0516	400	WALKER, GARY	1775.25
6340	100	POWERS, SUSAN	1725.00
5718	300	HART, BOB	1222.00

DPTMST File

The example Department Master File fields used in this text are the following:

Field Name	Field Description	Data Type
DPTNO	Department Number	three alphanumeric characters
DPTNAME	Department Name	20 alphanumeric characters
DPTBUDG	Department Annual Budget	seven numeric characters (an integer)

The data in the DPTMST file are the following:

DPTNO	DPTNAME	DPTBUDG
600	ADMINISTRATION	150,000
100	ACCOUNTING	75,000
500	MAINTENANCE	67,000
200	PAYROLL	342,500
400	COMPUTER SERVICES	750,000
300	PERSONNEL	56,000

ADRMST File

The example Employee Address Master File fields used in this text are the following:

Field Name	Field Description	Data Type
EMPID	Employee ID Number	four alphanumeric characters
STREET	Street Address	20 alphanumeric characters
CITY	City	15 alphanumeric characters
STATE	State	two alphanumeric characters
ZIP	Zip Code	five alphanumeric characters
PHONE	Telephone	10 alphanumeric characters

The data in the ADRMST file are the following:

EMPID	STREET	CITY	STATE	ZIP	PHONE
7290	610 WASHINGTON #6	BOSTON	MA	01002	6175339876
5718	7353 ADAMS AVE	PORTLAND	OR	97801	5038771275
1234	639 JEFFERSON #110	BOSTON	MA	01021	6175320888
2567	8462 CARTER BLVD	PORTLAND	OR	97811	5038774561
5632	4549 MADISON AVE	BOSTON	MA	01022	6175334702
3567	784 MONROE	PORTLAND	OR	97822	5038769455
4672	8462 JACKSON	BOSTON	MA	01022	6175338483
1892	8562 VAN BUREN	PORTLAND	OR	97827	5038763260
3516	4345 TYLER	BOSTON	MA	01025	6175331111
6340	2698 POLK	PORTLAND	OR	97812	5038773828

Displaying Physical File Data on the AS/400

To look at the data in a physical file member to which you have access authority, use the CL command, Display Physical File Member. For example,

Type	**DSPPFM**	on any command line
Press	**F4**	

See Figure A.1 for an example of this screen.

Figure A.1
Display Physical File Member (DSPPFM) Command Prompt Screen

```
                    Display Physical File Member (DSPPFM)
Type choices, press Enter.

File . . . . . . . . . . . . . . . ___________   Name
  Library  . . . . . . . . . . .     *LIBL       Name, *LIBL, *CURLIB
Member . . . . . . . . . . . . . .  *FIRST       Name, *FIRST, *LAST
From record  . . . . . . . . . . .  1




                                                                   Bottom
F3-Exit    F4-Prompt    F5-Refresh    F12-Cancel    F13-how to use ...
```

Type	**PAYMST**	as the file name
Type	**a library name**	if PAYMST is not in your library
Press	**Enter**	

You will see the information shown in Figure A.2.

Figure A.2
Display Physical File Member Screen, with Data

```
                          Display Physical File Member
File . . . . . :     PAYMST            Library . . . . . :     yourname
Member . . . . :     PAYMST            Record. . . . . . :     1
Control. . . . .                       Column. . . . . . :     1
Find . . . . . .
*...+....1....+....2....+....3....+....4....+....5....+....6....
1234400JONES, BILL           132200
3567600SMITHE, CAROL         156775
5632200GREEN, TOM            120000
2567100ADAMS, MARK           154650
4672600BLACKBERG, KAREN      130000
7290400KLEIN, JOHN           140000
1892500TUCKER, MARY          150000
0516400WALKER, GARY          177525
6340100POWERS, SUSAN         172500
5718300HART, BOB             122200
                             ****** END OF DATA ******

                                                                   Bottom
F3-Exit    F12-Cancel  F19-Left  F20-Right  F24-More keys
```

This is the PAYMST file data as it is stored on the AS/400. There are no spaces between fields. Note the position numbers in the line above the data.

Positions 1-4	employee ID
Positions 5-7	department number
Positions 8-27	employee name (The name field is 20 characters long.

	Any name that is fewer than the maximum number of characters is padded with trailing blanks.)
Positions 28-33	monthly salary

The decimal point for monthly salary is not stored in the record. The physical file record description describes the position of the assumed decimal point.

Appendix B

Collating Sequence and Processing Options

Selecting a Collating Sequence

A collating sequence is used by a computer for sorting records and comparing fields. The collating sequence assigns a value to every character. This concept was referenced in Chapter 6 in the discussion on the report summary functions of minimum and maximum. If you select the Select collating sequence option from the Define the Query menu, you will be permitted to change from the AS/400 default collating sequence of EBCDIC (hexadecimal) to another option.

One option is the English collating sequence. Lowercase and uppercase of the same letter of the alphabet are sorted, or compared, equally. If you remember, in the AS/400 default collating sequence, all lowercase letters sort before (lower than) all uppercase letters.

A second option is to create your own collating sequence for sorting or comparing. A third option is to define a translation table for the collating sequence.

For more information about selecting a collating sequence, see the *Query/400 User's Guide.*

Specifying Processing Options

The processing options help you to control the precision and accuracy of the query output. The first option is the use of rounding. The AS/400 default is rounding. All result fields, average and total summary functions, and overriding numeric field lengths on the Specify Report Column Formatting display will be rounded. This option can be changed to "no," which would result in truncation. Multiple rounding can cause mathematical errors, depending on your operations.

The second option is to ignore data decimal errors. These are run-time errors that occur when non-numeric data occurs in numeric fields. The AS/400 default is not to ignore data decimal errors and to abort your Query execution. This option can be changed if you know that your data is bad, but you still want to process the file.

The third processing option, to ignore character substitution warnings, is used with collating sequence translations. Refer to the *AS/400 Query User's Guide* for more information.

Appendix C

Date Processing

Introduction

Date processing functions are available in Query/400. The Define Result Fields screen is used to perform these manipulations. Some of the date operations available are adding years, months, and/or days to a date to determine a new date; subtracting two dates to determine the number of years, months, and days between the two dates; extracting the month, day, or year from a date field; and comparing a date to the current system date. The date field must be defined as a data type of DATE to use these result field functions.

If you are defining a record using Data Description Specifications (DDS), a date field is defined with a type of L, just as a character field is defined with a type of A. The date field is 10 characters formatted as YYYY-MM-DD.

If a date is not a DATE data type field, it must be converted to this data type before any of the Query date functions are used. The DATE function converts a character date in the AS/400 Job Date format to a DATE data type. The Job Date format is the system date format with separators; for example, MM/DD/YY.

TIP: Use F17 on the Define Result Fields display to see your system date format.

The format of the character date must match the AS/400 Job Date format for the conversion from character data type to DATE data type to work. The remainder of this appendix will assume that the Job Date is in MM/DD/YY format.

The following examples show how to convert numeric and character dates to a DATE data type.

Converting a Numeric Date

A numeric date data type must first be converted to a character date data type. (Then the character date will have the slashes inserted with the substring function.) The DIGITS function is used to convert a numeric data type to a character data type. For example, assume a record contains a numeric date field named HIREDT (hire date) with a format of YYMMDD. The following expression is used on the Define Result Fields display to convert this numeric date to a character date:

```
HIREDT1        DIGITS(HIREDT)
```

HIREDT1 is now a character data type, and can be manipulated with character operators.

Converting a Character Date

A character date must be in the correct job date format (MMDDYY) and contain slashes for the DATE function to convert this character data type to a DATE data type. If the format is not MMDDYY, the substring operator must be used to re-arrange the date. The concatenation operator is used to insert the slashes.

From the previous example, HIREDT1 is a character data type in the format YYMMDD. To convert HIREDT1 to the Job Date format MM/DD/YY, you would enter the following expression on the Define Result Fields display:

```
HIREDT2        SUBSTR(HIREDT1,3,2) || '/' ||
               SUBSTR(HIREDT1,5,2) || '/' ||
               SUBSTR(HIREDT1,1,2)
```

HIREDT2 is now a character data type of MM/DD/YY. HIREDT2 will be converted to the DATE data type using the DATE function with the following expression on the Define Result Fields display:

```
HIREDT3        DATE(HIREDT2)
```

You can now use HIREDT3 with any of the date functions on the Define Result Fields display.

Examples of Date Operations

We will use the following date data type fields and their corresponding values to demonstrate the date functions and arithmetic operations:

DATE1 — 12/01/92
DATE2 — 06/01/90
DATE3 — 01/05/93

The expressions will be shown as they would appear on a Define Result Fields display.

Date fields can be added to and subtracted from to create another date field. For example, the following expression,

```
NEWDATE        DATE3 + 30 DAYS
```

adds 30 days to the value 01/05/93. The result field NEWDATE would contain the value 02/04/93. DAYS is a function that can be used with a constant value.

DAYS can also be used to return a numeric representation of a date, in terms of days. For example, the following expression,

NUMDAYS DAYS(DATE3) - DAYS(DATE1)

subtracts 12/01/92 from 01/05/93 to determine the number of days between the two dates. The result field NUMDAYS would contain the value 35.

The functions MONTH, DAY, and YEAR return the month, day, and year portion of any date field. For example, the following expression,

NUMYRS YEAR(DATE1) - YEAR(DATE2)

would calculate the number of years between the two dates, 12/01/92 and 06/01/90, and place the value 2 in the result field NUMYRS. These same functions can also be used to extract the month, day, or year from a date field. Using the same dates as an example, the following expression,

EXTRACTMM MONTH(DATE2)

would result in the value 6 being placed in EXTRACTMM.

The function CURRENT can be used with the DATE function to find the value of the current system date. For example, if today is March 14, 1993, the following expression,

CURDT CURRENT(DATE)

would assign the value 03/14/93 to the field CURDT. This CURDT field can now be compared against other date fields. If DATE3 is 01/05/93, then in the following expression,

NUMDAYS DAYS(CURDT) - DAYS(DATE3)

NUMDAYS would be assigned the value 68. These last two expressions can also be combined into one expression by using the CURRENT function in the expression.

NUMDAYS CURRENT(DATE) - DAYS(DATE3)

For more information about date and time operations, see the *Query/400 User's Guide.*

Index

& (Ampersand), 52, 76
' (Single quote), 34-37
% (Percent sign), 35
_ (Underscore), 35
| (Vertical bar), 18-22

A

ADRMST data file, 82
Access path, 55, 78
Ampersand (&), 52, 76
AND/OR comparisons, 35
Arithmetic operators (EQ, NE, LT...), 34, 59, 85
Arrival sequence, 2, 25
Ascending sequence, 26
Authority (*LIBCRTAUT), 78
Average option, 42-44

B

Batch mode, 5, 6, 7, 68, 72
Break level (0 to 6), 48, 64
Break text — *See* Final totals

C

Case-sensitive operations, 34, 85
Character fields, 18
Collating sequence, 85
Column headings, 17-63
Column length, 63-69
Column spacing (between), 63, 64
Concatenation, 18-22, 69
Constants, numeric, 34
Control breaks, 47-53
Copies, number of, 74
Copying files — *See* CPYF command
Count option, 42-44
Cover page, 75, 76
CPYF (Copy File) command, 79
Create options, 3, 76
Current keyword, 89

D

Data, tip concerning, 15, 18, 19, 66, 68, 78
Data description specifications (DDS), 55, 63, 87
Data files, 81-84
Database files, 1, 31, 55-61, 72-76
Date and time fields, 15, 68, 75, 87-89
Date, time, and page, tip concerning, 76
Date keyword (&DATE), 87
Day keyword, 88
Date processing, 87
Decimal positions, 17, 44, 63
Define field names with joins, tip about how to, 59, 78
Descending sequence, 26
Detail data lines, 47,72
Digits keyword, 87
Display device, 72
Display physical file (DSPPFM), 82-84
Display the physical file member, tip about how to, 78
Displaying a physical file — *See* DSPPFM command
Dollar sign displays, 67, 68
DPTMST data file, 81
DSPPFM (Display Physical File) command, 78, 79, 82
Duplicate fields, tip concerning, 61

E

EBCDIC collating sequence, 43, 85
Editing numeric output fields, 63
Equal (EQ), 34, 59, 85; *see also* Arithmetic operators, Relational operators
Exit Query — *See* Query screens
Expand field information, tip about how to, 16, 27, 33, 52

F

Field, common keys, 55
Field considerations, 1, 16, 17, 63-65
Field ID, 55, 56
Field lengths of zero, 64
File identifier, 55-61
Files, 1, 4, 55-61, 72, 77
- type:
  - multiple input, 55-61
  - physical, 2, 3
  - QPQUPRFIL, 7, 13, 22, 28, 78
  - QRYDFN, 2
  - *QRYDFN, 2, 7
  - QSYSPRT, 79

Final totals, 50-52
Footings, 75, 76
Function keys
- F3, 5, 7
- F4, 7, 78
- F5, 5
- F9, 56
- F11, 16
- F12, 5
- F13, 18
- F16, 66, 68
- F17, 87
- F20, 11

G

Greater than or equal (GE), 34, 59, 85; *see also* Arithmetic operators, Relational operators
Greater-than sign, 4, 19
Greater than (GT), 34, 59, 85; *see also* Arithmetic operators, Relational operators

H

Headings, 75, 76

I

Inserting fields, 11
Interactive processing, 2, 5, 6

J

Joining files, 55-61
Joining with key fields, 59-61

K

Key fields, 55, 59

L

Less than or equal (LE), 34, 59, 85; *see also* Arithmetic operators, Relational operators
Less than (LT), 34, 59, 85
Library, 2, 3, 4, 77
LIBCRTAUT (Library Create Authority) command, 78
LIKE comparison, 34, 35
Line wrapping, 72, 73
LIST comparison, 34
Logical files, 55
Lowercase, 34

M

Major sort field, 26
Matched records, 57
Matched records with primary file, 58
Maximum option, 42-44
Message, 5, 7
Minimum option, 42-44
Minor sort field, 26
Month keyword, 89
More, 16, 33
Multiple files, 55-61

N

Negative sign choices, 67
None (*None), 65
Not equal (NE), 34, 59, 85; *see also* Arithmetic operators, Relational operators
Numeric fields and editing, 17, 65-69

O

Objects, 1
OR/AND comparisons, 35
Output Queue, 7, 72
Output field lengths, 63
Output formatting, 8

P

PAYMST data file, 81
Page breaks, 47, 48, 51
Page headings and footings, 71-76
Page keyword (&PAGE), 75
Page, cover, 75
Percent sign (%), 35

Q

Query screens:
- Define database file output, 77
- Define numeric field editing, 66-69
- Define printer output, 73
- Define report breaks, 3, 50, 64
- Define result fields, 3, 15, 16, 19, 20, 85
- Define spooled output, 74
- Define the Query 1, 3, 4, 5, 6, 10, 12
- Describe numeric field editing, 20, 67
- Display report 1, 5, 12, 20, 22, 26, 28, 38, 42, 44, 49, 52, 53
- Exit this Query, 6, 10, 12, 16, 26, 32
- Format report break, 50, 51
- Select and sequence fields 1, 3, 9, 10, 11, 21, 64
- Select collating sequence, 3, 85
- Select output type and output form, 3, 71-79
- Select records, 3, 33-40
- Select report summary function, 3, 42
- Select sort fields, 3, 25, 29, 48
- Specify cover page, 74, 75
- Specify file selections, 3, 4, 5, 56, 57
- Specify how to join files, 59
- Specify page heading & footing, 75
- Specify processing options, 3
- Specify report column formatting, 3, 63-69, 85
- Specify type of join, 58
- Spooled output, hold, 74
- Work with Queries, 2, 32

Quote mark ('), 34-37

R

RANGE comparison, 34
Records, 1, 2
Relational operators (EQ, NE, LT...), 58, 59, 85
Report breaks, 47-53
Resequence fields, tip about how to, 11
Result field naming conventions, 16
Return to default editing choices, tip about how to, 68
Return to default heading, tip about how to, 65
Rounding, 85

S

Saving and exiting, 5
Sort Priority — *see* Query screens, Select sort fields
Sort
- Major to minor fields, 26, 50
  - *see also* Query screens, Select sort fields

Space character, 34
Spacing for reports, 63, 73
Spooled output file, 72
Substring operations, 17-22, 69, 88
Substrings, tip concerning, 19
Summary data lines, 47
Suppress summaries option, 51; *see also* Average option, Count option, Minimum option, Maximum option, and Total option
Suppress summary information, tip about how to, 52

T

Time and date fields, 68, 75
Tips
- covering data, 15, 18, 19, 66, 68, 78
- covering date, time, and page, 76
- covering duplicate fields, 61
- covering substrings, 19
- covering undisplayed fields, 16, 33, 59, 60
- to define field names with joins, 59, 78
- to display the physical file member, 78
- to expand field information, 16, 27, 33, 52
- to resequence fields, 11
- to return to default editing choices, 68
- to return to default headings, 65
- to suppress summary information, 52

Titles for reports, 75
Total option, 42-44

U

Underscore (_), 35
Undisplayed fields, tip concerning, 16, 33, 59, 60
Unmatched records with primary file, 58
Uppercase, 34

V

Variable information in break text, 52
Vertical bar (|), 18-22

W

WRKOBJPDM (Work with Objects Using PDM) command, 7
WRKQRY (Work with Query) command, 2, 7, 9, 31
Wild-card characters, 35
Wrap-lines, 72

Y

Year keyword, 89

Also Published by *NEWS/400*

Visit our web site at **www.dukepress.com** for a more detailed listing of all Duke Press books

THE A TO Z OF EDI

By Nahid M. Jilovec

Electronic Data Interchange (EDI) can help reduce administrative costs, accelerate information processing, ensure data accuracy, and streamline business procedures. Here's a comprehensive guide to EDI to help in planning, startup, and implementation. The author reveals all the benefits, challenges, standards, and implementation secrets gained through extensive experience. She shows how to evaluate your business procedures, select special hardware and software, establish communications requirements and standards, address audit issues, and employ the legal support necessary for EDI activities. 263 pages.

APPLICATION DEVELOPER'S HANDBOOK FOR THE AS/400

Edited by Mike Otey, a **NEWS/400** *technical editor*

Explains how to effectively use the AS/400 to build reliable, flexible, and efficient business applications. Contains RPG/400 and CL coding examples and tips, and provides both step-by-step instructions and handy reference material. Includes diskette. 768 pages, 48 chapters.

AS/400 DISK SAVING TIPS & TECHNIQUES

By James R. Plunkett

Want specific help for cleaning up and maintaining your disk? Here are more than 50 tips, plus design techniques for minimizing your disk usage. Each tip is completely explained with the "symptom," the problem, and the technique or code you need to correct it. 72 pages.

AS/400 SUBFILES IN RPG

On the AS/400, subfiles are powerful and easy to use, and with this book you can start working with subfiles in just a few hours — no need to wade through page after page of technical jargon. You'll start with the concept behind subfiles, then discover how easy they are to program. The book contains all of the DDS subfile keywords announced in V2R3 of OS/400. Five complete RPG subfile programs are included, and the book comes complete with a 3.5" PC diskette containing all those programs plus DDS. The book is an updated version of the popular *Programming Subfiles in RPG/400.* 200 pages, 4 chapters.

C FOR RPG PROGRAMMERS

By Jennifer Hamilton, a **NEWS/400** *author*

Written from the perspective of an RPG programmer, this book includes side-by-side coding examples written in both C and RPG to aid comprehension and understanding, clear identification of unique C constructs, and a comparison of RPG op-codes to equivalent C concepts. Includes many tips and examples covering the use of C/400. 292 pages, 23 chapters.

CL BY EXAMPLE

By Virgil Green

CL by Example gives programmers and operators more than 850 pages of practical information you can use in your day-to-day job. It's full of application examples, tips, and techniques, along with a sprinkling of humor. The examples will speed you through the learning curve to help you become a more proficient, more productive CL programmer. 864 pages, 12 chapters.

CLIENT ACCESS TOKEN-RING CONNECTIVITY

By Chris Patterson

Attaching PCs to AS/400s via a Token-Ring can become a complicated subject — when things go wrong, an understanding of PCs, the Token-Ring, and OS/400 is often required. *Client Access Token-Ring Connectivity* details all that is required in these areas to successfully maintain and trouble-shoot a Token-Ring network. The first half of the book introduces the Token-Ring and describes the Client Access communications architecture, the Token-Ring connection from both the PC side and the AS/400 side, and the Client Access applications. The second half provides a useful guide to Token-Ring management, strategies for Token-Ring error identification and recovery, and tactics for resolving Client Access error messages. 125 pages, 10 chapters.

COMMON-SENSE C

Advice and warnings for C and C++ programmers

By Paul Conte, a **NEWS/400** *technical editor*

C programming language has its risks; this book shows how C programmers get themselves into trouble, includes tips to help you avoid C's pitfalls, and suggests how to manage C and C++ application development. 100 pages, 9 chapters.

CONTROL LANGUAGE PROGRAMMING FOR THE AS/400

By Bryan Meyers and Dan Riehl, **NEWS/400** *technical editors*

This comprehensive CL programming textbook offers students up-to-the-minute knowledge of the skills they will need in today's MIS environment. Progresses methodically from CL basics to more complex processes and concepts, guiding readers toward a professional grasp of CL programming techniques and style. 512 pages, 25 chapters.

DDS BY EXAMPLE

By R S Tipton

DDS by Example provides detailed coverage on the creation of physical files, field reference files, logical files, display files, and printer files. It includes more than 300 real-life examples, including examples of physical files, simple logical files, multi-format logical files, dynamic selection options, coding subfiles, handling overrides, creating online help, creating reports, and coding windows. 360 pages, 4 chapters.

DDS PROGRAMMING FOR DISPLAY & PRINTER FILES

By James Coolbaugh

Offers a thorough, straightforward explanation of how to use Data Description Specifications (DDS) to program display files and printer files. Covers basic to complex tasks using DDS functions. The author uses DDS programming examples for CL and RPG extensively throughout the book, and you can put these examples to use immediately. Focuses on topics such as general screen presentations, the A specification, defining data on the screen, record-format and field definitions, defining data fields, using indicators, data and text attributes, cursor and keyboard control, editing data, validity checking, response keywords, and function keys. A complimentary diskette includes all the source code presented in the book. 446 pages, 13 chapters.

DESKTOP GUIDE TO THE S/36

By Mel Beckman, Gary Kratzer, and Roger Pence, **NEWS/400** *technical editors*

This definitive S/36 survival manual includes practical techniques to supercharge your S/36, including ready-to-use information for maximum system performance tuning, effective application development, and smart Disk Data Management. Includes a review of two popular Unix-based S/36 work-alike migration alternatives. Diskette contains ready-to-run utilities to help you save machine time and implement power programming techniques such as External Program Calls. 387 pages, 21 chapters.

THE ESSENTIAL GUIDE TO CLIENT ACCESS FOR DOS EXTENDED

By John Enck, Robert E. Anderson, and Michael Otey

The Essential Guide to Client Access for DOS Extended contains key insights and need-to-know technical information about Client Access for DOS Extended, IBM's strategic AS/400 product for DOS and Windows client/server connectivity. This book provides background information about the history and architecture of Client Access for DOS Extended; fundamental information about how to install and configure Client Access; and advanced information about integrating Client Access with other types of networks, managing how Client Access for DOS Extended operates under Windows, and developing client/server applications with Client Access. Written by industry experts based on their personal and professional experiences with Client Access, this book can help you avoid time-consuming pitfalls that litter the path of AS/400 client/server computing. 430 pages, 12 chapters.

ILE: A FIRST LOOK

By George Farr and Shailan Topiwala

This book begins by showing the differences between ILE and its predecessors, then goes on to explain the essentials of an ILE program — using concepts such as modules, binding, service programs, and binding directories. You'll discover how ILE program activation works and how ILE works with its predecessor environments. The book covers the new APIs and new debugging facilities and explains the benefits of ILE's new exception-handling model. You also get answers to the most commonly asked questions about ILE. 183 pages, 9 chapters.

IMPLEMENTING AS/400 SECURITY, SECOND EDITION

A practical guide to implementing, evaluating, and auditing your AS/400 security strategy

By Wayne Madden, a **NEWS/400** *technical editor*

Concise and practical, this second edition brings together in one place the fundamental AS/400 security tools and experience-based recommendations that you need and also includes specifics on the latest security enhancements available in OS/400 Version 3 Release 1. Completely updated from the first edition, this is the only source for the latest information about how to protect your system against attack from its increasing exposure to hackers. 389 pages, 16 chapters.

INSIDE THE AS/400

An in-depth look at the AS/400's design, architecture, and history

By Frank G. Soltis

The inside story every AS/400 developer has been waiting for, told by Dr. Frank G. Soltis, IBM's AS/400 chief architect. Never before has IBM provided an in-depth look at the AS/400's design, architecture, and history. This authoritative book does just that — and also looks at some of the people behind the scenes who created this revolutionary system for you. Whether you are an executive looking for a high-level overview or a "bit-twiddling techie" who wants all the details, *Inside the AS/400* demystifies this system, shedding light on how it came to be, how it can do the things it does, and what its future may hold — especially in light of its new PowerPC RISC processors. 475 pages, 12 chapters.

AN INTRODUCTION TO COMMUNICATIONS FOR THE AS/400, SECOND EDITION

By John Enck and Ruggero Adinolfi

This second edition has been revised to address the sweeping communications changes introduced with V3R1 of OS/400. As a result, this book now covers the broad range of AS/400 communications technology topics, ranging from Ethernet to X.25, and from APPN to AnyNet. The book presents an introduction to data communications and then covers communications fundamentals, types of networks, OSI, SNA, APPN, networking roles, the AS/400 as host and server, TCP/IP, and the AS/400-DEC connection. 210 pages, 13 chapters.

JIM SLOAN'S CL TIPS & TECHNIQUES

By Jim Sloan, developer of QUSRTOOL's TAA Tools

Written for those who understand CL, this book draws from Jim Sloan's knowledge and experience as a developer for the S/38 and the AS/400, and his creation of QUSRTOOL's TAA tools, to give you tips that can help you write better CL programs and become more productive. Includes more than 200 field-tested techniques, plus exercises to help you understand and apply many of the techniques presented. 564 pages, 30 chapters.

MASTERING THE AS/400

A practical, hands-on guide

By Jerry Fottral

This introductory textbook to AS/400 concepts and facilities has a utilitarian approach that stresses student participation. A natural prerequisite to programming and database management courses, it emphasizes mastery of system/user interface, member-object-library relationship, utilization of CL commands, and basic database and program development utilities. Also includes labs focusing on essential topics such as printer spooling; library lists; creating and maintaining physical files; using logical files; using CL and DDS; working in the PDM environment; and using SEU, DFU, Query, and SDA. 484 pages, 12 chapters.

OBJECT-ORIENTED PROGRAMMING FOR AS/400 PROGRAMMERS

By Jennifer Hamilton, a **NEWS/400** *author*

Explains basic OOP concepts such as classes and inheritance in simple, easy-to-understand terminology. The OS/400 object-oriented architecture serves as the basis for the discussion throughout, and concepts presented are reinforced through an introduction to the C++ object-oriented programming language, using examples based on the OS/400 object model. 114 pages, 14 chapters.

PERFORMANCE PROGRAMMING — MAKING RPG SIZZLE

By Mike Dawson, CDP

Mike Dawson spent more than two years preparing this book — evaluating programming options, comparing techniques, and establishing benchmarks on thousands of programs. "Using the techniques in this book," he says, "I have made program after program run 30%, 40%, even 50% faster." To help you do the same, Mike gives you code and benchmark results for initializing and clearing arrays, performing string manipulation, using validation arrays with look-up techniques, using arrays in arithmetic routines, and a lot more. 257 pages, 8 chapters.

POWER TOOLS FOR THE AS/400, VOLUMES I AND II

Edited by Frederick L. Dick and Dan Riehl

NEWS 3X/400's Power Tools for the AS/400 is a two-volume reference series for people who work with the AS/400. Volume I (originally titled *AS/400 Power Tools*) is a collection of the best tools, tips, and techniques published in *NEWS/34-38* (pre-August 1988) and *NEWS 3X/400* (August 1988 through October 1991) that are applicable to the AS/400. *Volume II* extends this original collection by including material that appeared through 1994. Each book includes a diskette that provides load-and-go code for easy-to-use solutions to many everyday problems. *Volume I*: 709 pages, 24 chapters; *Volume II*: 702 pages, 14 chapters.

PROGRAMMING IN RPG IV

By Judy Yaeger, Ph.D., a **NEWS/400** *technical editor*

This textbook provides a strong foundation in the essentials of business programming, featuring the newest version of the RPG language: RPG IV. Focuses on real-world problems and down-to-earth solutions using the latest techniques and features of RPG. Provides everything you need to know to write a well-designed RPG IV program. Each chapter includes informative, easy-to-read explanations and examples as well as a section of thought-provoking questions, exercises, and programming assignments. Four appendices and a handy, comprehensive glossary support the topics presented throughout the book. An instructor's kit is available. 450 pages, 13 chapters.

PROGRAMMING IN RPG/400, SECOND EDITION

By Judy Yaeger, Ph.D., a **NEWS/400** *technical editor*

This second edition refines and extends the comprehensive instructional material contained in the original textbook and features a new section that introduces externally described printer files, a new chapter that highlights the fundamentals of RPG IV, and a new appendix that correlates the key concepts from each chapter with their RPG IV counterparts. Includes everything you need to learn how to write a well-designed RPG program, from the most basic to the more complex, and each chapter includes a section of questions, exercises, and programming assignments that reinforce the knowledge you have gained from the chapter and strengthen the groundwork for succeeding chapters. An instructor's kit is available. 440 pages, 14 chapters.

PROGRAMMING SUBFILES IN COBOL/400

By Jerry Goldson

Learn how to program subfiles in COBOL/400 in a matter of hours! This powerful and flexible programming technique no longer needs to elude you. You can begin programming with subfiles the same day you get the book. You don't have to wade through page after page, chapter after chapter of rules and parameters and keywords. Instead, you get solid, helpful information and working examples that you can apply to your application programs right away. 204 pages, 5 chapters.

THE QUINTESSENTIAL GUIDE TO PC SUPPORT

By John Enck, Robert E. Anderson, Michael Otey, and Michael Ryan

This comprehensive book about IBM's AS/400 PC Support connectivity product defines the architecture of PC Support and its role in midrange networks, describes PC Support's installation and configuration procedures, and shows you how you can configure and use PC Support to solve real-life problems. 345 pages, 11 chapters.

RPG ERROR HANDLING TECHNIQUE

Bulletproofing Your Applications

By Russell Popeil

RPG Error Handling Technique teaches you the skills you need to use the powerful tools provided by OS/400 and RPG to handle almost any error from within your programs. The book explains the INFSR, INFDS, PSSR, and SDS in programming terms, with examples that show you how all these tools work together and which tools are most appropriate for which kind of error or exception situation. It continues by presenting a robust suite of error/exception handling techniques within RPG programs. Each technique is explained in an application setting, using both RPG III and RPG IV code. 164 pages, 5 chapters.

RPG IV BY EXAMPLE

By George Farr and Shailan Topiwala

RPG IV by Example addresses the needs and concerns of RPG programmers at any level of experience. The focus is on RPG IV in a practical context that lets AS/400 professionals quickly grasp what's new without dwelling on the old. Beginning with an overview of RPG IV specifications, the authors prepare the way for examining all the features of the new version of the language. The chapters that follow explore RPG IV further with practical, easy-to-use applications. 500 pages, 15 chapters.

RPG IV JUMP START

Moving ahead with the new RPG

By Bryan Meyers, a **NEWS/400** *technical editor*

Introducing the "new" RPG, in which the columnar syntax has been challenged (all the specifications have changed, some vestigial specifications from an earlier era have been eliminated, and new specifications and data types have been added), this book shows you RPG IV from the perspective of a programmer who already knows the old RPG. Points out the differences between the two and demonstrates how to take advantage of the new syntax and function. 193 pages, 12 chapters.

RPG/400 INTERACTIVE TEMPLATE TECHNIQUE

By Carson Soule, CDP, CCP, CSP

Here's an updated version of Carson Soule's *Interactive RPG/400 Programming*. The book shows you time-saving, program-sharpening concepts behind the template approach, and includes all the code you need to build one perfect program after another. These templates include code for cursor-sensitive prompting in DDS, for handling messages in resident RPG programs, for using the CLEAR opcode to eliminate hard-coded field initialization, and much more. There's even a new select template with a pop-up window. 258 pages, 10 chapters.

S/36 POWER TOOLS

Edited by Chuck Lundgren, a **NEWS/400** *technical editor*

Winner of an STC Award of Achievement in 1992, this book contains five years' worth of articles, tips, and programs published in *NEWS 3X/400* from 1986 to October 1990, including more than 290 programs and procedures. Extensively cross-referenced for fast and easy problem solving, and complete with diskette containing all the programming code. 737 pages, 20 chapters.

STARTER KIT FOR THE AS/400, SECOND EDITION

An indispensable guide for novice to intermediate AS/400 programmers and system operators

By Wayne Madden, a **NEWS/400** *technical editor*

with contributions by Bryan Meyers, Andrew Smith, and Peter Rowley

This second edition contains updates of the material in the first edition and incorporates new material to enhance it's value as a resource to help you learn important basic concepts and nuances of the AS/400 system. New material focuses on installing a new release, working with PTFs, AS/400 message handling, working with and securing printed output, using operational assistant to manage disk space, job scheduling, save and restore basics, and more basic CL programming concepts. Optional diskette available. 429 pages, 33 chapters.

SUBFILE TECHNIQUE FOR RPG/400 PROGRAMMERS

By Jonathan Yergin, CDP, and Wayne Madden

Here's the code you need for a complete library of shell subfile programs: RPG/400 code, DDS, CL, and sample data files. There's even an example for programming windows. You even get some "whiz bang" techniques that add punch to your applications. This book explains the code in simple, straightforward style and tells you when each technique should be used for best results. 326 pages, 11 chapters, 3.5" PC diskette included

TECHNICAL REFERENCE SERIES

Edited by Bryan Meyers, a **NEWS/400** *technical editor*

Written by experts — such as John Enck, Bryan Meyers, Julian Monypenny, Roger Pence, Dan Riehl — these unique desktop guides put the latest AS/400 applications and techniques at your fingertips. These "just-do-it" books (featuring wire-o binding to open flat at every page) are priced so you can keep your personal set handy. Optional online Windows help diskette available for each book.

Desktop Guide to CL Programming

By Bryan Meyers, a **NEWS/400** *technical editor*

This first book of the **NEWS/400** *Technical Reference Series* is packed with easy-to-find notes, short explanations, practical tips, answers to most of your everyday questions about CL, and CL code segments you can use in your own CL programming. Complete "short reference" lists every command and explains the most-often-used ones, along with names of the files they use and the MONMSG messages to use with them. 205 pages, 36 chapters.

Desktop Guide to AS/400 Programmers' Tools

By Dan Riehl, a **NEWS/400** *technical editor*

This second book of the **NEWS/400** *Technical Reference Series* gives you the "how-to" behind all the tools included in *Application Development ToolSet/400* (ADTS/400), IBM's Licensed Program Product for Version 3 of OS/400; includes Source Entry Utility (SEU), Programming Development Manager (PDM), Screen Design Aid (SDA), Report Layout Utility (RLU), File Compare/Merge Utility (FCMU) — *new in V3R1*, and Interactive Source Debugger — *new in V3R1*. Highlights topics and functions specific to Version 3 of OS/400. 266 pages, 30 chapters.

Desktop Guide to DDS

By James Coolbaugh

This third book of the **NEWS/400** *Technical Reference Series* provides a complete reference to all DDS keywords for physical, logical, display, printer, and ICF files. Each keyword is briefly explained, with syntax rules and examples showing how to code the keyword. All basic and pertinent information is provided for quick and easy access. While this guide explains every parameter for a keyword, it doesn't explain every possible exception that might exist. Rather, the guide includes the basics about what each keyword is designed to accomplish. The *Desktop Guide to DDS* is designed to give quick, "at your fingertips" information about every keyword — with this in hand, you won't need to refer to IBM's bulky *DDS Reference* manual. 132 pages, 5 major sections.

Desktop Guide to RPG/400

*By Roger Pence and Julian Monypenny, **NEWS/400** technical editors*

This fourth book in the *Technical Reference Series* provides a variety of RPG templates, subroutines, and copy modules, sprinkled with evangelical advice, that will help you write robust and effective RPG/400 programs. Highlights of the information provided include string-handling routines, numeric editing routines, date routines, error-handling modules, tips for using OS/400 APIs with RPG/400, and interactive programming techniques. For all types of RPG projects, this book's tested and ready-to-run building blocks will easily snap into your RPG. The programming solutions provided here would otherwise take you days or even weeks to write and test. 211 pages, 28 chapters

Desktop Guide to Creating CL Commands

By Lynn Nelson

In this most recent book in the *Technical Reference Series*, author Lynn Nelson shows you how to create your own CL commands with the same functionality and power as the IBM commands you use every day, including automatic parameter editing, all the function keys, F4 prompt for values, expanding lists of values, and conditional prompting. After you have read this book, you can write macros for the operations you do over and over every day or write application commands that prompt users for essential information. Whether you're in operations or programming, don't miss this opportunity to enhance your career-building skills. 164 pages, 14 chapters.

UNDERSTANDING BAR CODES

By James R. Plunkett

One of the most important waves of technology sweeping American industry is the use of bar coding to capture and track data. The wave is powered by two needs: the need to gather information in a more accurate and timely manner and the need to track that information once it is gathered. Bar coding meets these needs and provides creative and cost-effective solutions for many applications. With so many leading-edge technologies, it can be difficult for IS professionals to keep up with the concepts and applications they need to make solid decisions. This book gives you an overview of bar code technology including a discussion of the bar codes themselves, the hardware that supports bar coding, how and when to justify and then implement a bar code application, plus examples of many different applications and how bar coding can be used to solve problems. 70 pages.

USING VISUAL BASIC WITH CLIENT ACCESS APIs

By Ron Jones

This book is for programmers who want to develop client/server solutions on the AS/400 and the personal computer. Whether you are a VB novice or a VB expert, you will gain by reading this book because it provides a thorough overview of the pinciples and requirements for programming in Windows using VB. Companion diskettes contain source code for all the programming projects referenced in the book, as well as for numerous other utilities and programs. All the projects are compatible with Windows 95 and VB 4.0. 680 pages, 13 chapters.